D1200473

ALASKA
A LAND IN
MOTION

Nancy Warren Ferrell

University of Alaska Fairbanks

Alaska Department of Education

Alaska Geographic Alliance

This book and its accompanying Teachers' Guide were produced as materials to help teach students in Alaskan elementary schools about the geography of their state. The work was funded by a grant from the Alaska Legislature, and was produced through the cooperation of the Alaska Department of Education; the University of Alaska Fairbanks, Department of Geography; and the Alaska Geographic Alliance, a statewide organization of educators and others supportive of geography education. The Alaska Geographic Alliance receives funding from the National Geographic Society and is housed at The Institute of the North in Anchorage.

Copyright ©1994 by the University of Alaska Fairbanks. Any views expressed or implied in this publication should not be interpreted as official positions of the University, the Alaska Department of Education, or the Alaska Geographic Alliance.

Alaska state and regional maps © Alaska Northwest Publishing Company and Raven Maps, 1992.

First Edition. Fourth printing, 2002

ISBN 1-887419-00-4

Alaska State Library Cataloging-In-Publication Data-

Ferrell, Nancy Warren,
    Alaska : a land in motion / Nancy Warren Ferrell —1st ed.
        p. cm.

    "...produced through the cooperation of the Alaska Department of Education; the University of Alaska, Fairbanks, Department of Geography; and the Alaska Geographic Alliance".
    Includes bibliographical references and index.

    1. Geography—Study and teaching (Elementary)—Alaska. 2. Alaska—Study and teaching (Elementary). 3. Education, Elementary—Alaska. I. University of Alaska, Fairbanks. Dept. of Geography. II. Alaska. Dept. of Education. III. Alaska Geographic Alliance. IV. Title.
LB158.F47 1994
372.891/09798

Project Administrator, **Roger W. Pearson**
Managing Editor, **Marge Hermans**
Graphic Design, **Elizabeth Knecht**
Pre-Press and Print Coordination, **Exact Imaging**

AGA

Alaska Geographic Alliance
935 W. Third Avenue
Anchorage, AK 99501
http://www.AK-Geo-Alliance.org

Institute of the North
Alaska Pacific University
P.O. Box 101700
Anchorage, AK 99510-1700
http://www.institutenorth.org

Grateful acknowledgment is made to the following for permission to reprint material copyrighted or controlled by them:

"Flood in Allakaket" from *Han Zaadlitl'ee*, Yukon-Koyukuk School District. Reprinted by permission.

"Why St. Lawrence Island is Called *Sivuqaq*" from *Kallagneghet/Drumbeats: A Reading Series in Yupik and English*. Reprinted by permission of Bering Strait School District.

From "The Ten-Legged Polar Bear" in *Northern Tales: Traditional Stories of Eskimo and Indian People*. Selected and edited by Howard Norman. Pantheon Books, A Division of Random House, Inc., 1990. Reprinted by permission.

Yupik Calendar from *Yup'ik Eskimo Dictionary* by Steven A. Jacobson. Alaska Native Language Center, 1984. Reprinted with permission.

Pictograph figures from "Ancient Aleut Rock Painting" in *The Alaska Journal*, Autumn 1971. Reproduced with permission of Alaska Northwest Publishing Company.

"Traditional Athabascan Uses of the White Spruce" and paragraphs on the brown bear's hide from *Make Prayers to the Raven* by Richard Nelson. University of Chicago Press, 1983. Reprinted by permission.

From "Taking Away by Owl" as told by Galushia Nelson, in *Eyak Legends of the Copper River Delta*. Compiled by John F.C. Johnson, ©Chugach Heritage Foundation, 1988. Reprinted by permission.

From the Tlingit myth "How the Fish Came Into the Sea," as told by Billy Wilson Senior, from *Indian Fishing* by Hilary Stewart © 1977. Original recording and transcript by kind permission of Paul Bragstad. Published by Douglas & McIntyre. Reprinted by permission.

From "Alaskan Highway: An Engineering Epic" by Froelich Rainey, and "Hunters of the Lost Spirit" from *National Geographic*. Reprinted by permission of the National Geographic Society.

From *Edwin Simon, Huslia: A Biography* ©Yukon-Koyukuk School District. Hancock House, 1981. Reprinted by permission of Yukon-Koyukuk School District.

The **cover photo** of Mount Augustine erupting was taken by Jürgen Kienle, a volcanologist and professor of geophysics at the University of Alaska, Fairbanks. Prof. Kienle took the photo while in a light plane flying upwind of the volcano during the eruption on March 31, 1986.

Title page photo: Bunchberries by Jim Hauck

Printed in Hong Kong

Table of Contents

PART 1 Alaska, A Landscape in Motion

AMNWR

PART 2 Alaska's People in Motion

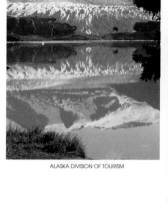

ALASKA DIVISION OF TOURISM

PART 3 Five Regions of Alaska Today

The Far North Region

The Western Region

ALASKA DIVISION OF TOURISM

The Interior Region

The Southcentral Region

The Southeast Region

ALASKA DIVISION OF TOURISM

List of Maps and Diagrams

Foreword

Many Americans think of Alaska as isolated in a remote corner of the world. In reality, it is right at the center of the world's land masses, as close to London and Tokyo as to New York.

As you will learn from this book, and as you study a globe, you will discover that our closest neighbors are not other states but other countries: Canada and Russia. Most Americans think Russia is half a world away. To us, it is within eyesight.

Here in the North, we don't look up. We don't look down. We look around. We have much to learn from our fellow Arctic regions and much to share. The day of the Arctic has come, and we have a great opportunity to help all Arctic peoples to learn from each other.

As the only Arctic state in the United States, we have often had to deal with national policies designed for the rest of the country, not for Alaska. These policies were born of misunderstanding, not malice. As Alaskans, our job is to educate America on our differences and opportunities. We live in an exciting place, filled with the glory of nature, a great variety of rich cultures, natural resources, and people who enjoy the challenge of adventure and pioneering.

I congratulate all those involved in writing, editing, and publishing this geography book. It will help our people of all ages to understand better the truth about this wonderful place where we live, with all of its potential, its opportunities, and its optimism.

Walter J. Hickel
Governor of Alaska
December 5, 1994

Danny Biggers, Stedman Elementary, Petersburg. Teacher Sally Riemer

Acknowledgments

Two Advisory Committees guided the creation of this book from its outset. The members included Teacher Consultants from the Alaska Geographic Alliance, representatives of various cultural groups, and other people committed to the support of geography education in Alaska. The committee members helped set educational goals and establish overall content of the book, and they were most helpful in reviewing drafts and contributing up-to-date information about the geography and the various regions of Alaska. The final product may not reflect their individual views, and any errors or omissions are the responsibility of the project team.

Advisory Committee Members

Roger Pearson, Fairbanks
committee co-chair

Marjorie Menzi, Juneau
committee co-chair

Mechelle Andrews, Gambell

Marie Angaiak, Fairbanks

Ronalda Cadiente, Juneau

Debbie Chalmers, Juneau

Richard Dauenhauer, Juneau

Bob Henning, Edmonds, WA

Janie Homan, Juneau

Kathy Itta, Barrow

Anne Kessler, Juneau

Janice Lund, Craig

Representative Terry Martin, Anchorage

Linda Munson, Barrow

Patricia Partnow, Anchorage

Dan Walker, Seward

Cal White, Fairbanks

No one writes and publishes a book alone. This project has benefitted from the generosity and good will of Alaskans from throughout the state. In particular the author would like to thank Roger Pearson and Marjorie Menzi, administrators of the project; Marge Hermans, managing editor; and Elizabeth Knecht, graphic designer. They provided not only expertise but ideas and materials as well. Without these people, the book would never have gotten off the geographic ground, let alone become published.

Besides members of the advisory committees, who provided comments and resources, others, including teachers, helped in varying degrees too numerous to mention. Special thanks go to Don Lynch of the University of Alaska Fairbanks, for his careful review of the text; Allan Cartography and Raven Maps for providing their beautiful topographic maps in page format; and Jim Fowler of Juneau for his colorful and creative illustrations.

Among the other people who deserve special thanks are: Stuart Allan, Lawrence Andreas, Jo Antonson, Nancy Babbitt, Artemis BonaDea, Charles Barnwell, Poppy Benson, Phyllice Bradner, Harvey Brandt, Diane Brenner, Bobbette Bush, Terri Campbell, Brenda Campen, Kathy Clark, Sue Cogswell, Dave Dossett, Robert DeArmond, Al Dekin, Rene Dolan, Alexander Dolitski, Linda Egan, Fairweather Forecasting, Ed Ferrell, Carmen Fields, Ellen FitzGerald, Bob Forbes, Jim Fowler, Ken Grant, Steve Henrickson, Mark and Audrey Hodgins, Gail Hollingsworth, John Holst, Helen Howard, Saundra Hutchins, Joyce Jennings, Larry Kaplan, Harold Kaveolook, Jürgen Kienle, Michael Krauss, Gladi Kulp, Dee Longenbaugh, Jody Marcello, Bill Martin-Muth, Lael Morgan, Laurie McNicholas, Claire Murphy, Susan Murphy, Bill Nash, Pam Odom, Tom Osborn, Tom Ostercamp, Barbara Page, Todd Paris, Naomi Pascal, Bill Paulick, Marlene Pearson, Jesse Pollard, Laura Lee Potrikus, Nancy Rabener, Loren Rasmussen, Jim Rea, Robin Renfroe, Penny Rennicke, Sigmund Restad, Malcolm Roberts, Charlotte Rowe, Jim Ruotsala, Bill Schneider, Robert Schroeder, Kay Shelton, Katy Spangler, India Spartz, Colleen Stevens, Peter Stortz, Greg Streveler, Kathy Sullivan, K.A. Swiger, Cornelia Thornton, Thomas Thornton, Les Viereck, Edith Vorderstrasse, Lynn Wallen, Rose Watabe, Deborah Watson, Sally Wiley, Greg Williams, Williwaw Publishing, Joanne Wilson, Denise Witte, Kes Woodward, Bill Workman, Bruce Wright, Charla Wright, and Louie Yannotti.

We also thank the teachers and parents who encouraged their students to contribute to this project; the photographers who generously submitted or provided photos; and the staffs of the school districts and various municipal, state, and federal agencies who helped us locate information, photos, and other resources, including the Alaska State Library, the Alaska State Museum, the Juneau Public Libraries, and the Alaska Maritime National Wildlife Refuge (AMNWR) in Homer; the Alaska Departments of Commerce and Economic Development, Education, Fish and Game, and Labor; the Alaska Division of Tourism; the Alaska Seafood Marketing Institute; the Alaska Native Language Center, the Alaska Oral History Center, and the Geophysical Institute at the University of Alaska Fairbanks; the Anchorage Museum of History and Art; the North Slope Borough; the U.S. Geological Survey in Juneau, the U.S. Forest Service, BLM Fire Service, U.S. Air Force, U.S. Coast Guard, U.S. Army Corps of Engineers, National Marine Fisheries Service, and National Weather Service.

Special thanks go to the students who helped with the project. Their geosketches, photos, and art work give a touch to the book that will speak most personally to other students.

Notes on Using This Book

Measurements

You can **convert** the U.S. measures used in this book to metric measures:

When you know	Multiply by	To find
feet	.3	meters
miles	1.6	kilometers
pounds	.45	kilograms

You can **estimate** how the U.S. measures used in this book will convert to metric measures:

Distances in feet will equal about one-third as many meters.

Distances in miles will equal about one and a half times as many kilometers.

Weight in pounds will equal a little less than half as many kilograms.

Temperatures throughout this book are given in degrees Fahrenheit (°F). If you want to know how degrees Fahrenheit compare with degrees Celsius, use a scale like this one:

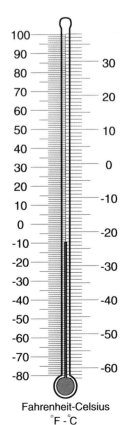

Fahrenheit-Celsius
°F - °C

Special Words

Words in this special type face are very important in the study of geography. They are explained in the **glossary** at the back of this book.

Some words are printed in this special type face to give them emphasis and make them stand out.

Suggested Reading

Books for further reading are listed at the ends of Part 1—Alaska's Landscape in Motion, and Part 2—Alaska's People in Motion, and at the end of each regional section in Part 3.

The sample of books selected for suggested reading are broad and varied because student interests are broad and varied. There are "read alone" and "read to" selections in both fiction and nonfiction. Where possible, the most current books were selected because they are still in print and carry up-to-date information. There are, however, other excellent new and old books that are timeless and should be included in geographic study.

Besides the author's knowledge, a bibliography developed by Dr. Katy Spangler of Eagle River, Alaska, was especially helpful in making these book selections.

RUSSIA

ARCTIC CIRCLE

CHUKO

CHUKOTSKIY
PENINSULA

BERING STRAI

NO

THE NORTHERN HEMISPHERE
North Pole to the Equator

ALASKA WORLD
This is the circumpolar rim of the
earth showing the countries also
sharing the lands above Latitude
50°N, which is Alaska's most
southerly point.

KUSKOKWIM

BRIST

BERING SEA

ALEUTIAN   ISLANDS   ALAS

PACIFIC

ARCTIC OCEAN

SEA

BEAUFORT SEA

BARROW

KOTZEBUE SOUND

BROOKS RANGE

ARCTIC CIRCLE

CANADA

WARD PENINSULA

SOUND

YUKON RIVER

KUSKOKWIM MTS

FAIRBANKS

DAWSON

YUKON RIVER

BETHEL

ALASKA RANGE

WRANGELL MTS

ANCHORAGE

CHUGACH MTS

WHITEHORSE

COOK INLET

KENAI PENINSULA

ST ELIAS MTS

PRINCE WILLIAM SOUND

BAY

PENINSULA

ALEUTIAN RANGE

SHELIKOF STRAIT

KODIAK ISLAND

GULF OF ALASKA

JUNEAU

ALEXANDER ARCHIPELAGO

COAST MTS

DIXON ENTRANCE

ALASKA

Jointly produced by the Alaska Geographic Society
and the Alaska Geographic Alliance, © 1992,
Alaska Northwest Publishing Company.

Base map © Raven Maps & Images, used by permission.

| 0 | 1000 | 2000 | 3000 | 4000 | 5000 | 6000 | feet |
| 0 | 305 | 610 | 914 | 1219 | 1524 | 1829 | meters |

OCEAN

PART 1

Alaska,
A Landscape in Motion

View from Capital School, Juneau

PAUL HELMAR, SOUTHEAST EXPOSURE

Looking Out Your Classroom Window

What do you see when you look out the window of your school classroom?

If you lived in Barrow, you would see the icy Arctic Ocean. Or from a school window in Fort Yukon, you might see the Yukon River sliding by. And from a school window in Anchorage, you would see the Chugach Mountains or the gray waters of Cook Inlet.

Geography is the study of the earth and the living creatures on it. It teaches you about mountains and islands. It looks at rivers, lakes, and oceans. It sees how land, water, and air on the earth affect the people, plants, and animals who live there. Elements of geography help you decide whether you should put on a coat when you go outside. They decide if you will hear the scream of an eagle or the bark of a seal.

When you are looking out your classroom window, everything is in place. The river and the ocean may move, but the tides and the river's flow have probably been the same since you can remember. The islands and mountains look still and permanent.

But don't think because mountains stay in the same place they are not changing. They are. Sunshine heats and cracks them. Rivers carve

Geography helps us understand why the world is the way it is.

AMNWR

17

Times change.
Places change.
Nothing stays the
same.

R. E. JOHNSON

their sides. Winds whip over them. Plants sink roots, and animals burrow holes into them. Changes are going on all the time.

As the earth changes, people change, too. When winter winds blow, people don't put on swimming suits. They wear jackets—unless they fly to Hawaii for vacation! You can't walk on a river in the summer, but you can in the winter when it is frozen. Your family may have a cabin or fish camp in one place, but if the nearby river changes course, you may have to move.

Times change, places change, people change, weather changes. Nothing stays the same.

Geography helps you understand your world and how it changes. It helps you understand why people everywhere live the way they do. Geography is not like a jigsaw puzzle with separate little pieces. It is instead a flow, where one change affects another, no matter where you live in the world.

Weather changes, too.

DOUGLAS YATES

18

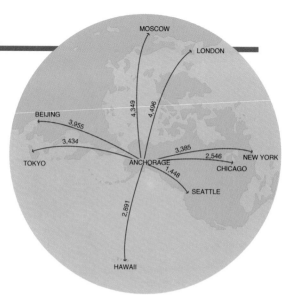

1 Focusing in on Alaska

Suppose you are in a space shuttle high in the air on a clear day. You know you are north of the Equator, flying over the North American continent. You are headed toward the North Pole. Your captain tells you to look down on Alaska.

Alaska's Location

FAIRWEATHER FORECASTING

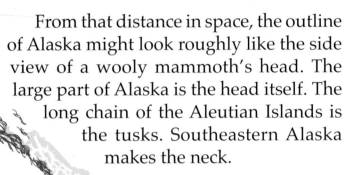

From that distance in space, the outline of Alaska might look roughly like the side view of a wooly mammoth's head. The large part of Alaska is the head itself. The long chain of the Aleutian Islands is the tusks. Southeastern Alaska makes the neck.

Over the top of the "head" might be great slabs of ice in the Arctic Ocean. Surrounding the face and the tusks, and along the neck is the Pacific Ocean. Almost touching the forehead is the country of Russia. A sprinkling of islands lie close to the face and under the tusks. At the back side of the head and neck is the country of Canada.

You know Alaska is large because you have flown over Texas, and the land you are looking at is twice as big. You check your atlas. Yes, Alaska covers 591,004 square miles to be exact.

"Take a reading on Anchorage," your captain says. "Latitude 61 degrees north. Longitude 150 degrees west. We'll bring her in at Elmendorf Air Force Base."

The shuttle banks right and loses altitude. As you zero in on Elmendorf, you see the rough mountains lining the wooly mammoth's face and running down the tusks. You see green valleys between. You see the white of glaciers over the mouth and under the chin.

As you drop closer and closer, your view narrows. It seems only water is below. This is the Gulf of Alaska, your map tells you.

Alaska's Neighbors

Nearing land, you follow Cook Inlet. It leads directly into the mammoth's mouth. And there, below, is Anchorage. You land at Elmendorf.

Once on the field, you notice the two flags flying overhead. One is the Stars and Stripes of the United States. The other is the Alaska flag. On the dark blue background its gold stars form the Big Dipper, like the star form you see in the sky. The seven Dipper stars on the flag point toward the North Star in the corner. You recognize the North Star immediately. You remember your training. Instruments brought you in to Elmendorf, but the North Star helped to guide you here.

Alaska is a land of variety. It is the biggest, the wildest, the flyingest, the farthest north state of the United States. Besides people of different cultures, it has mountains, valleys, tundra, islands, glaciers, and rivers.

Before looking at the land and waters of Alaska, let's consider two conditions many Alaskans live with every day—weather and permafrost.

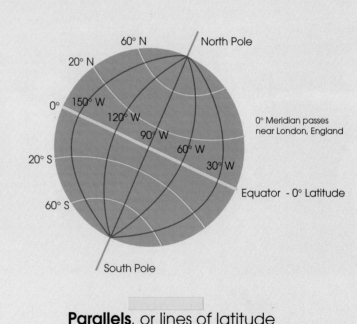

Latitude and Longitude

60° N
North Pole
20° N
0°
150° W
120° W
90° W
60° W
30° W
20° S
60° S
South Pole

0° Meridian passes near London, England

Equator - 0° Latitude

Parallels, or lines of latitude

Meridians, or lines of longitude

2 Alaska's Climates

When you went outside today, what did you wear? A jacket, a sweater, a slicker, a heavy parka? Maybe you walked to school in only a shirt and jeans. Of course, it depends on whether it is winter or summer.

Weather is what it's like outside where you live. Each day it's either wet or dry, cold or warm, windy or calm. *Climate* draws a picture of what weather is like over many years. Climate tells what a place is like most of the time.

Weather and climate depend on where you live and what time of year it is.

USDA FOREST SERVICE, JUNEAU

Every day you have to deal with weather. For instance, you would probably need a sweater in Nome even on the warmest day of summer. If you lived in Ketchikan, it might be a good idea to wear rain gear to school, especially during October. That's the rainiest month. On the other hand, if you lived in southern Arizona, you might never need a heavy sweater during the daytime for the whole year. Of course **weather** can fool you, but **climate** describes weather **most** of the time.

In the farthest north part of Alaska is the Arctic climate zone. In Barrow, for instance, students wear jackets almost every day of the year. Temperatures normally go only as high as 50°F during the summer. Of course some days

22

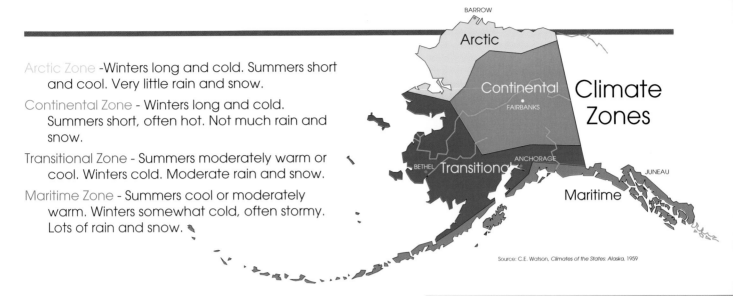

Arctic Zone -Winters long and cold. Summers short and cool. Very little rain and snow.

Continental Zone - Winters long and cold. Summers short, often hot. Not much rain and snow.

Transitional Zone - Summers moderately warm or cool. Winters cold. Moderate rain and snow.

Maritime Zone - Summers cool or moderately warm. Winters somewhat cold, often stormy. Lots of rain and snow.

Climate Zones

BARROW

Arctic

Continental

FAIRBANKS

BETHEL Transitional

ANCHORAGE

JUNEAU

Maritime

Source: C.E. Watson, *Climates of the States: Alaska*, 1959

could get warmer than that. Winter temperatures are often 25 or 30 degrees below zero (°F). There's not much rain or snow there, but the wind blows most of the time.

Winds, anywhere, make the air colder. If the temperature is 0°F, a 20-mile-an-hour wind can make it feel like minus 40°F. At that temperature, it wouldn't take long to get a frost-bitten nose.

The tipping of the earth affects Alaska's climates, especially in northern parts of the state. In winter, days are short, and less sunshine warms the earth. People in Barrow don't see the sun for more than two months in the winter.

In summer, the long days bring warmth and a burst of plant growth. It stays light outside for almost three months, day and night. Sorry, that should be day and **day.** There is no "night" at all. The constant light during the summer is the reason northern Alaska is often nicknamed "The Land of the Midnight Sun."

NANCY RABENER

In the Arctic climate zone winters are very cold, and the wind is often fierce. The ocean is frozen during many months of the year.

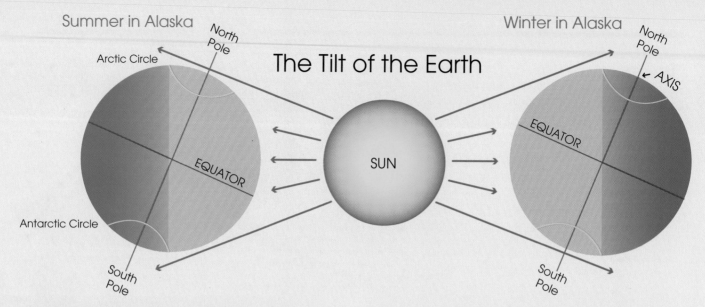

Alaska is colder than many other places partly because of its location on the earth.

The earth leans, or tilts, as it makes its long journey around the sun. The earth has an imaginary line going through it from north to south. Scientists call this line the earth's *axis*. The tilt of this axis causes the ends of the earth to receive different amounts of light and warmth from the sun.

When the North Pole is tipped toward the sun, the lands around it, such as Alaska, receive more hours of daylight. At the same time, these lands also receive more warmth from the sun. It is summer.

When the North Pole is tipped away from the sun, the lands around it have shorter days. The sun's rays are farther away. These lands are then colder. It is winter.

Usually ocean water mellows the temperatures of nearby land. However, in the Arctic the warmth and moisture of ocean waters do not count as much. Why? Because water in arctic oceans is so cold, and it is covered most of the year with ice. This northern section of Alaska stays cold and dry.

Traveling toward the south, we find the **Continental** climate zone in the middle of Alaska. Here, away from the coasts, it is land, rather than ocean, that most affects climate. Mountains rimming this central part of Alaska protect it from rain, so it is dryer. Temperatures in this inland climate zone vary a lot more.

Hours of Daylight in Four Cities

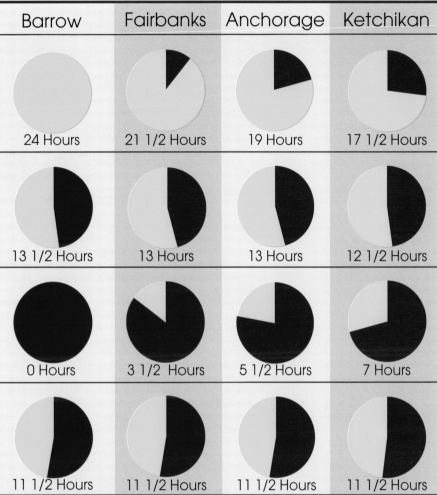

	Barrow	Fairbanks	Anchorage	Ketchikan
June	24 Hours	21 1/2 Hours	19 Hours	17 1/2 Hours
September	13 1/2 Hours	13 Hours	13 Hours	12 1/2 Hours
December	0 Hours	3 1/2 Hours	5 1/2 Hours	7 Hours
March	11 1/2 Hours	11 1/2 Hours	11 1/2 Hours	11 1/2 Hours

Source: Figures from the Alaska Division of Tourism.

Daylight
Darkness

Temperatures in the Continental zone can be very high or very low, depending on the season. The record high and the record low for Alaska were recorded in this interior area. The record high was 100°F at Fort Yukon in 1915. The record low was minus 80°F at Prospect Creek in winter, 1971. That's a difference of 180°F! Not many places in the world range that much.

Most thermometers can't even record such low temperatures. During Alaska's Gold Rush, miners could get a general idea of how cold it

DOUGLAS YATES

Cold, dry winters and powdery snow make for outdoor fun in the Continental climate zone.

The Transitional climate zone is affected by both the ocean and the land. Near the Aleutian Islands the weather is often stormy.

J. PENNELOPE GOFORTH

was by using quicksilver, or mercury. This is a liquid metal that always freezes at minus 40°F. When quicksilver froze, people had to be very careful they didn't freeze, too.

The miners found that having cold temperatures wasn't all bad. Sometimes they put a flat piece of ice over their cabin windows for glass, using wooden buttons to keep it in place. The window never melted until spring, and it never gathered frost. It was always clear.

In the Continental climate zone, summer daylight does not last as long as in the Arctic zone. But some days are quite long. In fact, just for fun, sport fans in Fairbanks play baseball on June 21, the longest day of summer. That's not odd by itself, but these teams play the game at midnight! What other baseball team can do that—without field lights?

Farther south near Anchorage and along the Bering Sea coast is the **Transitional** climate zone. Both the ocean and the land affect this climate type. Weather there is not as dry, or as extremely hot and cold, as in the Continental zone. However, it is not as wet or warm as in the southern Maritime zone either. Summer temperatures are in the 50s and 60s. Winter days average near 0°F.

The **Maritime** climate zone is the mildest in Alaska. It stretches eastward from the Aleutian Islands, around the Gulf of Alaska coast, and down throughout southeastern Alaska.

Maritime climate is moderated by the ocean. The ocean current from Japan warms the region even more. Average summer temperatures are about 60°F. Winters are quite mild, with temperatures in the 20s and 30s.

Places in Alaska with Maritime climate are rainy. They may have more than 100 inches of rain and snow a year. That's because moisture in the air is carried eastward from the Pacific Ocean. Moisture falls as rain at sea level, or as snow on cooler mountain tops. In the mountains, the snow feeds glaciers and ice fields. If it's warm enough at sea level, the rain and mild temperatures nourish lush coastal forests. Many parts of southeastern Alaska are covered by such dense *rainforests*.

You might think there would be rainforests on the Aleutian Islands, too. After all, they have a Maritime climate just as southeastern Alaska does. But that's not the case. The storm-lashed, windswept Aleutians have no trees at all. That is probably because of their constant stormy winds and steep cliffs.

While climate affects life above ground in Alaska, another condition affects life from underground.

The Water Cycle

Clouds rise, cool, and drop their water vapor as rain or snow.

The water vapor forms clouds.

Rain and melting snow fill the rivers and return to the ocean.

Water evaporates from the ocean.

Sitka black-tailed deer thrive in the lush forests of southeastern Alaska, a part of the Maritime climate zone.

R. E. JOHNSON

3 Permafrost

In very cold regions of the world, it is not just lakes and rivers that freeze. Soil holds water and freezes, too. Rocks and soil freeze together like cement.

If you were to dig into the ground near Barrow in the summer, this would happen: First the shovel would slide through thick tundra vegetation, then through wet soil, then—CLUNK!—it would smack into ice. Your shovel would not dig down any farther.

Almost 80 percent of Alaska has some *permafrost*, or ground that is frozen all year. At Barrow, the vegetation and upper soil, called the **active layer,** freezes in the winter and thaws out in the summer. Under that, only about a foot below the surface, is permafrost.

Near Fairbanks, where summers are warmer, permafrost begins about five feet below the surface. Around Palmer, which is near Anchorage and has an even milder climate, there is almost no permafrost at all.

You can't build anything right on top of permafrost. Well, you can, but if you don't take special care, you are in for surprises.

ROGER W. PEARSON

Permafrost is ground that is frozen all year long. The top, or **active layer,** may freeze in winter and thaw in summer. The lower, **inactive layer**, never thaws. Sometimes permafrost pushes up and breaks the surface of the soil, making a **permafrost boil,** like the one shown in this photo.

Permafrost shapes the land slowly and quietly. When permafrost near the ground's surface freezes and thaws over many years, it can crack the ground and form patterns called **ice-wedge polygons.** You can see these polygons in the ground in this photo taken near Prudhoe Bay. Freezing in permafrost areas can also make **pingos,** ice mounds covered with soil that grow several feet high.

ROGER W. PEARSON

Suppose you did. Suppose you built a school gym right on top of frozen ground. Soon the warm floor would melt the frozen ground under the gym. The ground outside would become mushy. It would no longer be hard enough to support the gym floor. Before long, the center of the gym floor would start sinking into the melting mushy ground underneath. The floor would no longer be even. Try playing basketball on a floor like that!

It's all right to build on permafrost if workers insulate first. If they use some kind of insulation between the permafrost and the building, the ground stays cold, even though the building above is heated.

ELDON THOMPSON, UAF GEOPHYSICAL INSTITUTE

This cut away bank shows permafrost.

Now to the grandest subjects of Alaska's geography, the features of land and water. Few places on earth compare with them.

Let's begin at the top of the world.

Permafrost in Alaska

■ Continuous permafrost

■ Permafrost in some places

■ Little or no permafrost

Source: Stuart A. Harris, *The Permafrost Environment*, 1986.

DOUGLAS YATES

Summer is growing time for animals and plants on the northern tundra.

In late summer berries are juicy and ripe on the northern tundra. People, birds, and other animals eat their fill and set aside extra for the winter

NANCY RABENER

4 Tundra

There is a frozen desert in Alaska's far north.

Areas in the far north are affected by the earth's tilt on its axis. Summers are very short, although daylight may be 24 hours long. Temperatures can rise to 70°F and 80°F. However, usually it's cooler. During winter, the thermometer may dive to minus 70°F, and there may be no daylight at all. There is very little rain throughout the year. This creates a kind of landscape known as *tundra*.

Tundra rose
TOM ELEY

Perhaps you think nothing grows on this frozen desert. But during the 24-hour daylight of summer, an explosion of color breaks out on the tundra. More than 900 kinds of mosses, sedges, lichens, grasses, flowers, and berries grow in the few thawed inches on the surface. Most of the roots do not grow down, but **sideways** in the soil. Plants manage to flower, seed, and then hang on through the winter for the next summer of growth.

Insects, too, like the tundra. Water trapped on top of frozen ground forms small pools and bogs where insects can breed. In summer, flies and mosquitoes explode in clouds. And where there are insects and plants, there are bound to be birds and other animals.

Bird Migration

Migrating birds such as ducks, geese, swans, and shore birds do not have maps to guide them, but these birds know where the tundra is. They seem to know it has lots of food, good places to nest, and long daylight hours. Every summer they arrive on the tundra by the thousands to mate, nest, and raise their young. Then they head south before the cold, dark winter comes.

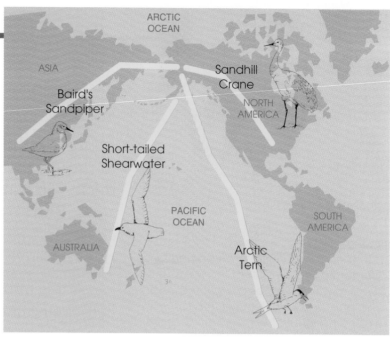

Source: Susan Quinlan and Lori Quakenbush, Alaska's Birds: Their Identification, Biology, and Conservation. A Guide for Youth Groups. Alaska Department of Fish and Game and University of Alaska Cooperative Extension Service, 1986.

The arctic tern, for one, is a flying champion. It spends seven months of the year traveling! The tern flies south to the Antarctic when there is summer there, then returns up north for the summer in Alaska. It may travel 22,000 miles round trip every year.

Another migrating bird is the Pacific golden plover. Plovers spend their winters in Hawaii as some Alaskans do, but these birds nest on the northern tundra in summer. Every fall plover families have to fly from Alaska to Hawaii, nearly 3,000 miles, nonstop over the ocean. And that's when the young birds are only three months old!

Warm-blooded animals such as arctic hares and arctic foxes live on the tundra. So do polar bears, snowy owls, and ravens.

Tundra swans usually nest in the grass near water. They lay three or four eggs. Mates often stay together for life.

ALASKA DEPT. OF FISH & GAME, JOHN HYDE

AMNWR, ROBERT ANGELL

In the fall, arctic foxes shed their brown summer coats. White winter fur helps **camouflage** them amid the snow. It is shed for brown fur again in the spring. The photographer caught this fox changing its coat in between seasons.

ALASKA DIVISION OF TOURISM

When they are threatened, musk oxen crowd together in a line or circle, facing outward. This is an effective defense against their primary enemy, the wolf. Their long, thick fur protects them against wind and cold. Inupiaqs call them *oomingmak,* "the animal with skin like a beard."

Marmots and ground squirrels curl up in dens during winter. Lemmings tunnel under the snow and feed on plants there during the dark months.

All tundra animals have thick fur or feathers to protect them from the cold. Musk oxen have thick, soft hair beneath their long-haired outer coat. Ptarmigan, sometimes called "tundra chickens," have leggings of feathers that grow right down to their toenails.

A few animals are especially *camouflaged* to help them stay alive. The arctic hare, which makes a tasty morsel for foxes, grows a white coat in winter. Matching the snow helps it hide from *predators*. But, alas, the arctic fox changes its brown summer coat for winter white, too—the better to sneak up on the camouflaged hare! White coats can work both ways.

Caribou, too, roam the tundra, traveling constantly to find enough food. They are often bothered by the mosquitoes and biting flies. Sometimes they stand in snowfields or climb to higher ground to escape the small pests.

Other animals such as Dall sheep, moose, gray wolves, and grizzly bears roam fringes of the tundra or live in *alpine tundra* high in the mountains.

Speaking of mountains, now let's look at these grand peaks of Alaska geography.

5 Mountains

Some third grade students attending Harborview Elementary School in Juneau were asked the question, "When you went to the Lower 48 states after living in Alaska, how were places different?"

One boy who had flown to visit his grandparents, described Florida. "It's so flat," he said.

That student was used to Alaska's mountains. Gigantic, snow-capped peaks are often the first thing people notice when they travel to Alaska.

When you fly north from Seattle, the Coast Mountain Range trails for hundreds of miles below. These are the highest coastal mountains in the world. Some peaks are 15,000 to 18,000 feet high. That's only a few thousand feet below Mt. McKinley, the highest peak in North America.

The Coast Mountains mark the boundary between Alaska and Canada. On the Canadian side is Mt. Logan, the second highest peak in North America.

These tall boundary mountains are one reason why southeastern Alaska is so rainy. Moisture from the Pacific Ocean rises into the air, moves inland, bumps into the mountains, and dumps rain on southeastern Alaska. The rain and mild climate make for heavy brush and thick forests of spruce and hemlock trees. Bears, mountain goats, and deer roam the area.

JOHN TUCKEY

Alaska has some of the most rugged mountains in all of North America. This is Troublemint Peak in the Talkeetna Mountains.

Dall sheep live on the ridges, meadows, and steep slopes of Alaska's mountains.

ALASKA DIVISION OF TOURISM

JOSE L. BOUZA, Courtesy KATHY SULLIVAN

Way To Go!

Twelve-year-old Taras Genet of Talkeetna, Alaska, did it!

Here Taras looks down on ALL of North America as he stands at the top of Mt. McKinley, the highest peak on the continent. The youngest mountaineer ever to make the summit, Taras reached the top with his party in June 1991. The climb took 17 days of struggling up, and one long day coming down. Even during the worst climbing sections, Taras knew he would never give up.

What was the hardest part of the trip? Maybe being away from home. And, Taras added, sometimes being with grownups all the time.

The coastal mountains then arch through the southcentral part of Alaska. There they are called the Alaska Range. These mountains build higher as they stretch inland and rise to the highest point in North America, Mt. McKinley. This high peak is called Denali ("The Great One") by some people, though the official U.S. name is Mt. McKinley. The peak itself rises to 20,320 feet. Mountaineers from all over the world want to climb to the top as a challenge, and a thousand of them try every year.

From Mt. McKinley, the coastal mountain system then drops south and west. There most of its tallest peaks rise above the ocean as the Aleutian Island Chain. Some of the stormiest weather in the world meets against these peaks. The North Pacific Ocean and the Bering Sea clash here. Stormy weather and rough waters are

The Aleutian Islands are the tops of an underwater mountain range about 1,400 miles long.

AMNWR, E. BAILEY

Alaska's Floating Plates

The earth's crust, all around the world, is made up of about 15 gigantic rocky plates. If you dug straight down, they would be maybe 25 miles deep.

These huge plates rest upon the hot, gummy *mantle* of the earth. When the earth's crust was being formed, these plates moved, sometimes spreading apart and sometimes grinding together. At times the pressure of their movements forced melted rock up through the earth's crust like toothpaste squeezed from a tube. That made mountains on land, or dug deep ditches such as the Aleutian Trench in the ocean floor.

These plates still move all the time, though maybe only a couple of inches a year. That's not much, but it can cause great changes. It can cause earthquakes, volcanic eruptions, and *tsunamis* on the surface of the earth. Alaska has all of those.

Aleutian Trench

Gulf of Alaska

Pacific Plate

North American Plate

Mantle

terrific problems for ships. Sea mammals, such as whales, seals, and sea otters, however, thrive in the waters off the islands.

Seabirds such as murres, gulls, and petrels flock to the Aleutian cliffs in huge colonies. Few land animals live there, although caribou, foxes, and reindeer have been brought there by people.

Some of these Coastal, Alaska, and Aleutian peaks are "young" and still growing. They are *volcanoes*, and sometimes they blow their tops. The southern area of Alaska from Sitka through the Aleutians is part of the "Ring of Fire." This ring is an arc of volcanoes rimming much of the Pacific Ocean.

A hard cooked egg has layers somewhat as the earth does.

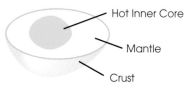

Hot Inner Core

Mantle

Crust

Cracked pieces of the egg's shell are somewhat like the earth's plates.

Concept from *Earthquakes: A Teacher's Package for K-6*. National Science Teachers Association, 1988.

The Ring of Fire

Alaska's volcanoes are part of the "Ring of Fire." The "ring" is an unstable part of the earth's crust that almost completely surrounds the Pacific Ocean. About half of Alaska's 80 volcanoes have let off steam or erupted in the last 130 years.

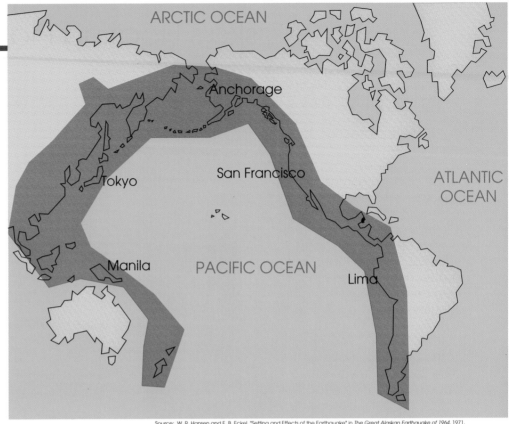

ARCTIC OCEAN

Anchorage

Tokyo

San Francisco

ATLANTIC OCEAN

Manila

PACIFIC OCEAN

Lima

Source: W. R. Hansen and E. B. Eckel, "Setting and Effects of the Earthquake" in *The Great Alaskan Earthquake of 1964*, 1971.

MARK AND AUDREY HODGINS

In April 1990, Redoubt Volcano erupted, throwing ash 15,000 to 20,000 feet into the air. Redoubt Volcano is on the west side of Cook Inlet and about 40 miles away from the towns of Kenai and Soldotna.

The *eruption* of volcanoes is caused by the restless shifting of oceanic and continental plates. This shifting releases molten rocks and gases that explode through the earth's crust.

Mt. Katmai north of Kodiak had the biggest eruption of any Alaskan volcano. That happened in 1912. In fact, Katmai's explosion was 70 times greater than Washington State's Mt. St. Helens eruption in 1980.

In northern Alaska, another long range of mountains extends across the state. The Brooks Range runs 720 miles east to west from Canada to the Chukchi Sea. The range is named for Alfred Hulse Brooks (1871-1924), a geologist who did much work in Alaska. This group of mountains continues the Rocky Mountain system that runs north through the western United States.

The long Brooks Range forms the southern border of arctic Alaska. The mountainsides facing north are almost bare, with few trees. The warmer southern sides grow more trees and plants. Temperatures are changeable. Summery warm days in the 70s can be followed by blizzards and cold.

A passage through these mountains—Anaktuvuk Pass—is one spot where herds of caribou pass each year. Every spring gigantic herds travel hundreds of miles to have their calves on the tundra to the north. Wolves follow closely at their heels. Grizzly bears, Dall sheep, and smaller animals, too, roam the mountains, brushy slopes and tundra of the Brooks Range country.

Mountains throughout Alaska provide recreational activities such as skiing, hiking, hunting, and fishing. Mountain land set aside for national wildlife parks protects the animals and allows people to watch and photograph them.

People are not interested in just the tops or the outside of mountains. Prospectors have dug **into** Alaskan mountains searching for gold. Other miners have also looked for valuable minerals such as zinc, copper, or nickel.

From Alaska's high mountains, now let's drop down the slopes to lower country and see what's there.

JOHN TUCKEY

Alaskans and visitors often go to the mountains to ski.

Much of Alaska's interior is covered by **boreal forest**. Trees grow best in the river valleys, but with harsh winters, none of them grow very big.

6 Rivers, Valleys, and Plateaus

The interior parts of Alaska, between the Brooks Range and the Alaska Range of mountains, are mainly valleys and raised flatlands called *plateaus*. Permafrost lies under the soil in many areas.

Much of interior Alaska is covered with *boreal forest*. Black spruce, tamarack, willow, and alder trees grow near patches of flat, boggy ground called *muskeg*. On higher ground, there are stands of white spruce, aspen, and birch trees. Permafrost and long winters do not allow trees to grow very big when you compare them with trees in a coastal forest.

Black bears, grizzly bears, and moose roam the hillsides. Smaller animals such as marten, wolverine, mink, and lynx hunt the region. A number of people in this part of Alaska trap animals for their fur.

Alaska has many important rivers. The five longest ones are:
1. Yukon   1,875 miles
   (about 1,400 miles in Alaska)
2. Porcupine 555 miles
   (about 185 miles in Alaska)
3. Koyukuk   554 miles
4. Kuskokwim 540 miles
5. Tanana   531 miles

Source: A Photographic Geography of Alaska. *Alaska Geographic*. Vol 7 No. 2. 1980.

A great number of important rivers flow through interior Alaska. There are the Yukon, the Porcupine, the Koyukuk, the Kuskokwim, and the Tanana. Rivers and their valleys are important in other parts of the state, too. More than one-third of all the fresh water in the United States flows in Alaska's rivers.

People in Alaska have always used rivers for highways. There were no roads in the old days, and there are very few roads in much of Alaska today. Over the centuries, people settled and built villages near rivers. They travel the rivers to reach hunting grounds, berry patches, fish camps, and summer cabins. They also travel them to reach neighboring villages, and they fish in them for food or for fun.

In winter most Alaskan rivers freeze over. Then they are roads for dog sleds, snowmachines, or even cars and trucks. People have to be careful, though. The ice is not always very thick.

In the spring when the river ice breaks up, huge blocks of ice grind noisily together, push each other high in the air, and sometimes cause floods. It is a dangerous time to be on any river.

Great numbers of salmon *spawn*, or lay their eggs, in rivers all over the state. Other fish such as trout, whitefish, sheefish, and pike live in the rivers, too. In winter, people fish through the ice for cod, burbot, pike, and trout.

ALASKA DIVISION OF TOURISM

Spawning salmon travel hundreds of miles up Alaskan rivers. They provide food and jobs for many Alaskans.

39

When Rivers Run Wild

CHRISTOPHER SIMON

In 1994, late summer rains caused the Koyukuk River to swell and overflow its banks. The water raged through several villages, including Hughes, shown in the photo to the left.

The village of Allakaket was also flooded. Niki Acker, a seventh grader, wrote about the flood for her school district newsletter, *Han Zaadlitl'ee*. She said: "It was very scary to see the houses, the store, and the hall float away. The water messed up everything and the gas station. We can't drink the water because it is very dirty. We had to travel by boat from the school to the helicopters to be rescued…. It was pretty weird to see boats go down where we used to walk on the roads."

All the waterways in Alaska are important, but none can outdo the mighty Yukon River. It is the major route for interior Alaska.

The Yukon River, flowing from plateaus in Canada, is the longest river in the state. It runs 1,400 miles in Alaska and more than 400 miles in Canada. It is the fourth longest river in North America.

The Yukon has many moods as it moves across Alaska. At times it rushes along between tall cliffs. At other times it barely moves as it swings back and forth on itself across flat lowlands. In western Alaska it rolls through wetlands until it reaches the Bering Sea. Where it enters Alaska from Canada, the government has saved land for falcons, waterfowl, and other animals in the Yukon-Charley National Monument.

The mighty Yukon River flows 1,400 miles across Alaska and more than another 400 miles in Canada.

STEVE KESSLER

In the western wetlands, south of Norton Bay, the Yukon spreads out into lowlands. There it meets the lowlands of another large river, the Kuskokwim. These marshy lands are important "resorts," where visiting geese, swans, cranes, and ducks come to spend the summer. Here the birds mate, raise families, and then leave before winter comes.

ALASKA DIVISION OF TOURISM, ROBERT ANGELL

Snow geese flock near the Stikine River on their way to and from their nesting grounds on the arctic slope.

Mink, beaver, moose, wolverine, and fox live near the wetlands areas, and grizzly bears roam these areas, too.

While we are looking at Alaskan waters, let's study another fresh water feature of geography—the lakes.

Water often collects and forms a lake at the end, or **terminus,** of a glacier. This is Portage Glacier lake near Anchorage.

ROGER W. PEARSON

7 Lakes

There are more than three **million** lakes in Alaska!

Many Alaskan lakes were formed by glaciers. Others formed from snow or rain draining from mountains. Where there is permafrost, *thaw lakes* may form when the permafrost melts near the surface. This melted water cannot drain into the frozen soil beneath. Anything from a puddle to a lake stays on top.

DOUGLAS YATES

Many lakes in northern Alaska are very shallow. They rest on top of frozen ground.

Lake Iliamna in western Alaska is the largest lake in Alaska. Two other lakes—Becharof on the Alaska Peninsula, and Teshekpuk in the Arctic—are big, but they are still only half the size of Iliamna. This largest lake covers 1,000 square miles.

To get an idea of how large that is, leave Alaska for a minute and fly to Europe. Pick up the small country of Luxembourg (north of France), fly back to Alaska, and put it in Lake Iliamna. Luxembourg would fit, and there would still be a little water around the edges of the country.

Iliamna is the second largest freshwater lake that is completely within the borders of the United States. Lake Michigan is the first.

If you ever fly over Iliamna, look under the surface for a huge, swimming shadow. There might, just might, be a monster living in the depths! People have reported seeing a "large unknown creature" or a "big, snake-like form" swimming in the lake. This is something like the "Loch Ness monster" people report seeing in Scotland. Maybe it's just for fun, but maybe not. Take a look.

The waters of Lake Iliamna and its nearby cousin, Lake Clark, feed many plants in the area. They provide water and healthy surroundings for muskrats, beavers, moose, grizzly and black bears, red foxes, caribou, and weasels. Birds, including ptarmigan, eagles, loons, snipes, and geese either visit or live along their shores. People use the lakes for boating and fishing, too.

ALASKA DIVISION OF TOURISM

Lake Clark is one of Alaska's prime fishing areas.

Rivers feed into lakes, and lakes spill out into rivers and then the ocean. Because of this, the Lake Iliamna area is one of the most important in the world.

You might know that salmon return to deposit their eggs in the freshwater river or lake where they began. There the eggs hatch and the young fish live the first part of their lives. Red salmon (also called "sockeye") that hatch in Lake Iliamna travel down to the ocean to grow. After a few years they come back to the lake and its nearby streams to spawn.

Lake Iliamna and nearby Lake Clark, which flow out to the ocean at Bristol Bay, have the largest runs of red salmon in the world.

The next time you open a can of red salmon for a sandwich, just think: That fish might have hatched several years earlier in Lake Iliamna.

Or, if someone has caught the monster in the meantime, that can might contain…

After traveling on the inland waters of Alaska, let's look at another kind of "river"—rivers of ice.

Hanging glaciers drape themselves over steep ledges high in the mountains.

JOHN TUCKEY

8 Glaciers, Rivers of Ice

Alaska has far more glaciers than any other state—about 100,000 altogether. Thousands of years ago glaciers covered about half of Alaska. Now they cover only a small portion of the state. Every mountain range in Alaska has them. Most glaciers, however, are in the southern part of the state.

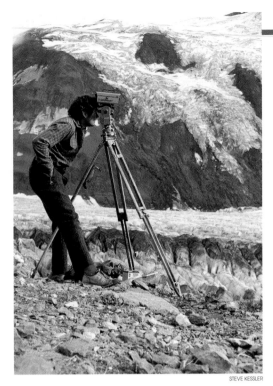
Scientists learn about glaciers by monitoring ice movement.

STEVE KESSLER

There are different kinds of glaciers. For instance, there are **hanging glaciers** high on mountainsides, **valley glaciers** that nestle between mountains, and **tidewater glaciers** that flow to the sea.

Glaciers spill from high mountains like frozen rivers. Some flow together and spread into a single, broad river of ice. The black stripes on the glacier's surface are dirt and stones picked up as the glacier scrapes along the land. If you count the black stripes, you can tell how many glaciers came together to form that one broad ice river.

Glaciers are formed when snow gathers on mountaintops and in high valleys. When the snow of one season does not melt before the next winter, more snow gathers there. After many years and layers of snow, a glacier is formed.

It is interesting how a glacier grows and moves.

Alaska's Glaciers

Malaspina is the largest glacier in North America. It is larger than the state of Rhode Island.

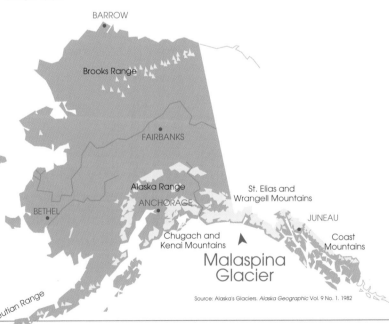

Source: Alaska's Glaciers. *Alaska Geographic* Vol. 9 No. 1. 1982

First, think of all the years of snow gathering in an area. This piling snow of a glacier gets heavy and presses on the layers of snow underneath. At last, all the air is squeezed out, and the snow turns to ice. Glacier ice is packed so tight, it lasts a long time. For instance, if you put a piece in a glass of soda pop, it lasts a lot longer than regular ice cubes do. After ice in a glacier has piled into layers many feet high, it gets so heavy it begins to flow down the mountain. It becomes a moving "river of ice."

When a glacier flows down the mountain, it digs and grinds into the rocks beneath. It carries rocks and boulders along and scrapes them against its bottom and sides.

As the heavy glacier moves forward, or **advances,** over many centuries, it carves a valley. If it melts back, or **retreats,** it leaves behind piles of dirt and rocks called a *moraine.*

STEVE KESSLER

Glaciers flow like frozen rivers, scraping rocks and earth along their sides as they move along.

A number of the best known glaciers are in Glacier Bay National Park in the St. Elias Mountain Range of southeastern Alaska. There are 13 active glaciers there. Often glaciers and inlets bear the names of people who helped explore the area. There are names such as Charley, Toyatte, and Muir.

R. E. JOHNSON

In 1986, Hubbard Glacier surged forward almost a mile in nine months. It formed a huge ice dam that broke the day after this photo was taken.

Harbor seals love the cold water and floating ice chunks near some glaciers. The floating ice makes a safe place for seals to rest and rear their young.

R. E. JOHNSON

Most of these glaciers are not flowing forward, however. They are **retreating,** or melting back. To give you an idea of how much, think of this. In the middle 1700s—about the time the United States became its own country—glaciers filled Glacier Bay. There was no place for boats to enter. Today, only about 200 years later, the glaciers are back 60 miles from the bay opening.

Every once in a while, certain glaciers may start moving forward very fast. These are called **surge glaciers**.

An interesting surge glacier is Hubbard Glacier in the Wrangell-St. Elias Mountains near Yakutat. It was named to honor the first president of the National Geographic Society, Gardiner Greene Hubbard (1822-1897). The glacier has been moving forward from Canada for 100 years. In 1986, prodded by a branching glacier higher up, the Hubbard advanced at a terrific rate for a glacier. It advanced almost a mile in nine months.

The Hubbard pushed forward, plugging a nearby saltwater inlet. Salt water in the inlet mixed with fresh water from rain and glacier melt. The water in the inlet began to rise about a foot a day. Soon the plugged waters of the inlet had risen 80 feet above sea level. When the ice dam finally broke, water exploded from the inlet. It burst out 35 times faster than the flow of Niagara Falls in New York State!

Animals such as harbor seals love the icy waters near glaciers. These creatures raise their young among the icebergs at the glacier's face. Overhead, gulls and puffins fly, living on the land close by.

Now let's look at another land feature where there are glaciers and seals, too. This geographic spotlight would focus on the islands of Alaska.

9 Islands

Islands are land areas with water all around them. There are so many small islands in Alaska, some have never been named.

Islands come in all sizes. Some are only a few rocks grouped together, and some are as big as Alaska's Kodiak Island. Kodiak Island has 3,588 square miles. That's almost the size of the entire state of Connecticut. The second largest island in Alaska is Prince of Wales Island. Prince of Wales is almost one-third smaller than Kodiak, with only 2,231 square miles.

When people hear the name Kodiak, they think of the giant brown bears living there. Some of these bears stand nine feet tall. They can weigh up to 1,500 pounds—about as much as three snowmachines! People like to photograph the bears, or hunt them for trophies. They also visit the island for sport and commercial fishing.

ROLLO POOL

Alaska's islands come in many sizes. Some, like most islands in southeastern Alaska, are covered with forests.

St. Matthew Island is far offshore in the Bering Sea.

AMNWR, V. BYRD

An Island Legend

The people of St. Lawrence Island have a legend about how their special island came to be, and why it is called by the name of *Sivuqaq*.

Anders Apassingok from Gambell shared this story with us:

After the Creator made the earth, He rested. While He rested, He looked over his creation and saw great emptiness upon those waters. So He reached out and put his hand into those waters and scooped up a handful of dirt from the ocean floor.

He then squeezed the water from the dirt. He set it on top of the empty waters and it became an island. In time, sod began to form on the island. From this rich growth grew life such as grass, plants, flowers, and roseroots, and willow leaves.

Mice, squirrels and foxes came to the island, lived on it and made it their home. Whales, walruses, seals, sea lions, and polar bears came to the coastal waters around the island. Some of the animals migrated while others stayed all year round. Some also came on the ocean ice in winter.

During the spring all kinds of birds came, built their nests, and laid their eggs. Some of the birds stayed the whole year round.

As time went on, people found the island. They settled on it and made it their home.

The shape of the island looks as if it was squeezed or wrung out with one hand.

So that is why it is called *Sivuqaq*, a word that means something "squeezed" and formed by the Creator.

Story from *Kallagneghet/Drumbeats*. Courtesy of the Bering Strait School District.
Map by Joy Silook, Naomi Booshu, Channa Koozaata, Gambell Elementary School. Teachers Mechelle Andrews and Peter Sutch

There are other large islands scattered along Alaska's coast. Off the western coast is Nunivak Island, where people have started herds of reindeer and musk oxen. North of Nunivak is larger St. Lawrence Island, where Siberian Yupik people have their homes.

The Aleutian Islands make up the tusks of the mammoth's head you imagined to represent Alaska. Strung out over 1,400 miles, they are the longest chain of small islands in the world. (Did you notice that if the Alaskan part of the Yukon River were stretched out straight, it would be the same distance?) The most westerly island of the Aleutians is Attu. If you took a ship and sailed directly south from Attu, you would land in New Zealand. Look at a map, and you'll see that both are at the same longitude.

You will remember that the Aleutians do not have any trees, but whales, sea otters, and seals make the waters around the islands their world headquarters.

Most of the Aleutian Islands have volcanoes. The islands are located along the deep underwater Aleutian Trench, and they have more than their share of earthquakes and tsunamis.

Look at a map again and notice how much of southeastern Alaska is made up of islands. Some larger ones are Baranof, Admiralty, and Chichagof. The largest of all, Prince of Wales Island, is the third largest island in the United States.

Every summer thousands of fur seals crowd the beaches of St. Paul Island, one of the Pribilof Islands off the west coast of Alaska. Aleut people harvest some of the seals for their pelts.

JIM HAUCK

JOHN TUCKEY

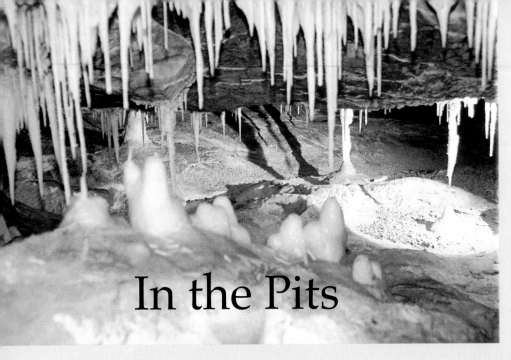

In the Pits

hole in the rock with water rushing through it. I named it Roaring Road Cave because it was roaring right by the road.

Once my dad found some giant bones preserved in a cave. Scientists dug them up and found that they were from a 12,000-year-old grizzly bear skeleton.

My name is Jedediah Smith. I am 10 years old. I live in Southeast Alaska, on Prince of Wales Island. The most fun thing I do is caving. North Prince of Wales is made mostly of limestone formed millions of years ago by coral reefs. The limestone has moved this far north by *plate tectonics*.

PHOTOS PETER SMITH

There are more than 200 caves in our area and a lot more that haven't been discovered yet. Caves are all different. The deepest pit in Alaska is El Cap Pit, 599 feet straight down. There are many small caves, too. You need special equipment to cave safely.

About a year ago I discovered a new cave. I was walking up the road and all of a sudden I heard this big roaring sound. Mom said it was just the wind. I went down to look. I saw a big

Jed Smith, Alyeska Central School. Teacher Debbie Chalmers

Some caves have beautiful formations. Formations have different names. "Moon milk" (which looks like cottage cheese) and "soda straws" (tiny transparent straws) are my favorites. Formations are very fragile. You should never touch one because you could break it or get it dirty, which would stop its growth.

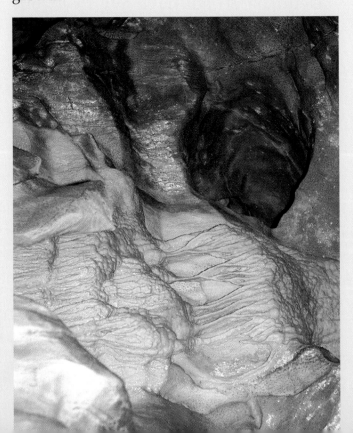

Unusual caves have been found on Prince of Wales Island at the north end near Whale Pass. In fact, the deepest cave of that type in the United States is there.

Most southeastern islands are mountainous and covered with rainforest. The sheltered waters around them are a playground for fish, whales, and seals—and people, too!

You can learn lots more about the oceans and seas around Alaska and its islands. Let's look at them now.

10 Oceans and Seas

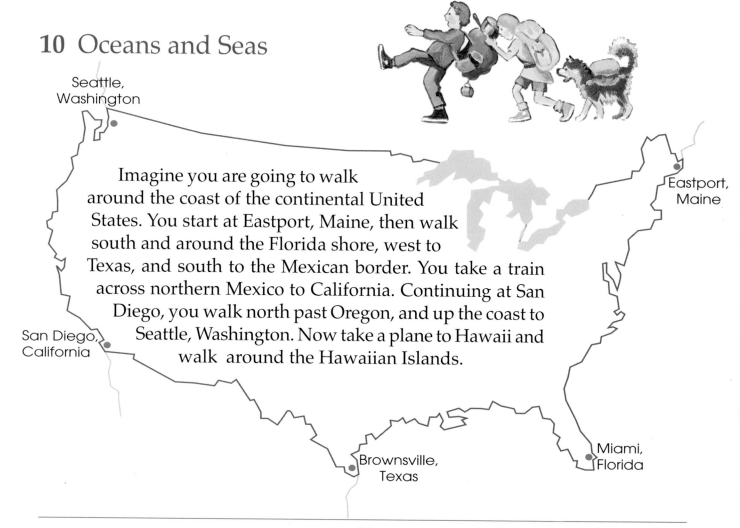

Imagine you are going to walk around the coast of the continental United States. You start at Eastport, Maine, then walk south and around the Florida shore, west to Texas, and south to the Mexican border. You take a train across northern Mexico to California. Continuing at San Diego, you walk north past Oregon, and up the coast to Seattle, Washington. Now take a plane to Hawaii and walk around the Hawaiian Islands.

Seattle, Washington

Eastport, Maine

San Diego, California

Brownsville, Texas

Miami, Florida

Math Challenge — Alaska's Coastline

You are probably tired after walking around the continental U.S. and Hawaii, so sit down and see if you can figure this out:

The Alaska coastline is 6,640 miles long. Suppose you walked 20 miles a day. How long would it take you to walk all around Alaska?

If you did the same amount of walking around the Alaska coast, you still wouldn't be done! The Alaska coastline is 6,640 miles long. That is about 900 miles longer than the coastline of all of the other 49 states.

Alaska is really a large *peninsula* surrounded on three sides by water. Two oceans form along its coasts, the North Pacific and the Arctic. Bays, inlets, sounds, and straits pattern the shoreline.

Above the head of the Alaska mammoth you have pictured in your mind is the Arctic Ocean. Parts of the Arctic Ocean—the Chukchi and the Beaufort Seas—wash northern and western shores. Giant slabs of pack ice form there nearly all year around.

Pack ice almost covers the surface of the Arctic Ocean. In summer, this ocean ice melts back. In winter, it freezes toward shore. Ice also forms from the land out into the ocean. In cold weather when the ocean ice collides with the expanding land ice, pressure forces the ice high into the air. The force builds ridges. Some of them are 12 feet high!

As the winter weather gets colder, the ocean freezes down

AMNWR, ELAINE RHODE

Alaska's coasts are washed by some of the most productive ocean waters in the world. For centuries many Alaskans have made their living from the sea.

Math Challenge Answer: 332 days, or almost a year

along the northwestern coast of Alaska, too. Among broken pieces of the ice, or *ice floes*, seals and walrus make their home. Sometimes the ice floes are several miles across. Polar bears use smaller floes as stepping stones to hunt the seals.

Farther west in the Arctic Ocean, about where the mammoth's forehead would be, continues the Chukchi Sea. Kotzebue Sound takes a large bite from land at that point. You can't draw a line where the Arctic Ocean stops and the Pacific begins, but the Chukchi Sea ends at the Bering Strait. There the continents of Asia and North America almost meet. Big Diomede Island, Russia, and Little Diomede Island, Alaska, are only a few miles away from each other.

The Bering Sea of the Pacific Ocean extends south along Alaska's western coast. It runs from offshore of the Seward Peninsula to the Aleutian

ALASKA DIVISION OF TOURISM

Polar bears live mostly near the sea ice. There, they hunt seals and sometimes walrus and whales. A polar bear may lie waiting for its prey for hours, camouflaged amid the ice and snow by its white coat.

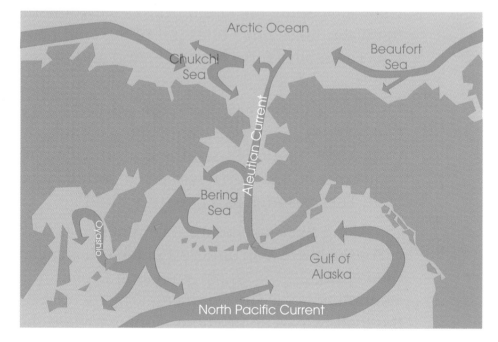

Ocean Currents

53

The Ocean Shrinks and a "Bridge" Appears

Who would ever think of an ocean shrinking? But it can.

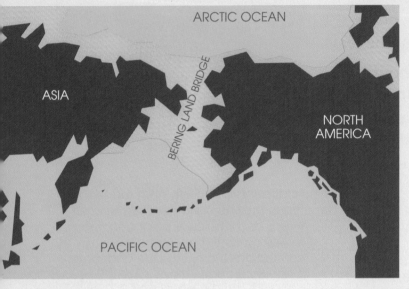

Thousands of years ago, much of Alaska was covered by glaciers. When that happened, a lot of ocean water was locked up in snow and ice. Because of this, the ocean water level dropped. Not much. Maybe about 500 feet. But it was enough to expose edges of land along the coast.

One shallow area exposed was the underwater land between Russia and Alaska. Scientists call it the Bering Land Bridge. It was about 1,000 miles wide. This wide "bridge" of land allowed animals and people from Asia to cross into North America.

In the thousands of years since then, temperatures around the world have warmed. Sheets of ice on land have melted. Water has drained back into the ocean. Ocean levels have risen again. Now water covers the area where the land bridge used to be.

Islands. Shaping the face of Alaska's mammoth, the water takes huge bites out of the land here, too. These bites form Norton Sound and Bristol Bay.

Alaska's southern shores are washed by the Gulf of Alaska, under the chin of the mammoth. Gulf waters are often wild and stormy. Waves sometimes 50 feet high have been reported in the Gulf. That's as high as a five story building.

Along the coasts of most continents, as well as Alaska, there is an underwater table. It is called the *continental shelf*. In your mind, picture a swimming pool. The continental shelf would be the shallow part along shore, sloping toward the

The Continental Shelf

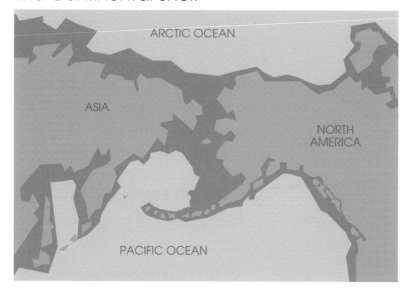

JIM HAUCK

Millions of plants and animals live in Alaska's oceans and seas. This sea star uses hundreds of tube-like feet on its underside for traveling and capturing *prey*.

Halibut fishing is very important in Alaska. Most halibut are caught on "skates," long lines with hundreds of hooks on them. The largest ever caught weighed nearly 500 pounds.

deep end. Sometimes it is a narrow strip, as around Africa. Sometimes it is wide and covers miles under the ocean surface.

Alaska is lucky. There is continental shelf all around the coastline of Alaska. An especially wide area is beneath the Bering and Chukchi Seas. That is where the Bering Land Bridge used to be.

This underwater "shallow table," close to the surface, receives a lot of sunlight in summer. Its cold waters hold more oxygen and healthier ingredients than warm waters, and ocean currents mix them around. Because of this, Alaska's table can grow many tiny plants and animals. These living things provide food for larger creatures.

JIM NILSEN

Tsunami!

U.S. COAST GUARD

Scotch Cap Lighthouse, Aleutian Islands

It was an April night in 1946.

The U.S. Coast Guard watchman at Scotch Cap lighthouse on Unimak Island yawned and stretched. He peered outside. Everything was black, the weather clear and calm for a change.

At that same moment, thousands of feet below the Pacific Ocean, a part of the Aleutian Trench fell away. The shift sent shock waves exploding through the ocean floor. The force moved low and fast in the water.

As the wave neared land, it roared and climbed in the shallow water. Higher and higher it rose until it towered 100 feet over the Unimak beach. Tons of water crashed against the lighthouse, pushing, smashing, and then pulling away the lighthouse and its five Coast Guard keepers to a watery death.

With such a table full of food, guess who comes to dinner? Seals, and sea lions, and walruses, and whales, and salmon, and halibut, and herring, and crabs, and shrimp, and so many other kinds of fish and animals. Bears, eagles, sea gulls, and other land and air creatures wait close by for their share. And so do people who go fishing.

This Bering Sea fishing area is shared with Russia, Japan, and other countries. Scientists know this section of the continental shelf is about 1,000 miles wide, and goes out from land about 500 miles. At that size, the area is a little smaller than the mainland of Alaska itself. That is a very, very big dining table!

On the south side of the Aleutian Islands is the underwater Aleutian Trench. The Trench is like a long trough, or ditch, about 100 miles wide and 2,000 miles long. At that spot under the ocean, two geologic plates meet. One plate plunges under the other. This unsteady region causes underwater earthquakes and tsunamis. Such a tsunami washed away Scotch Cap lighthouse on Unimak Island, in April of 1946.

Now that you know about the geographic features of Alaska, let's see how people fit in with them. A story about an ancient family will help take you back to earlier days.

NANCY RABENER

Alaska's landscape is rich and varied. So are the ways people found to make their homes in it.

Suggested Reading

Brandenburg, Jim. *To the Top of the World.* N.Y.: Walker and Co., 1993.

   A wildlife photographer films a pack of Arctic wolves on Ellesmere Island in Canada.

Cobb, Vickie. *This Place is Cold.* N.Y.: Walker and Co., 1989.

   The land, animals, plants, and climate of Alaska, are presented as a cold land.

Cole, Joanna. *The Magic School Bus on the Ocean Floor.* N.Y.: Scholastic, 1992.

   Ms. Frizzle takes her class on the magic school bus to the ocean floor where they learn about the waters and the creatures that live there.

Gill, Shelley. *Thunderfoot.* Homer, Alaska: PAWS IV Publications, 1988.

   Describes different prehistoric animals that lived in Alaska, and their environment.

Miller, Debbie S. *A Caribou Journey.* Boston: Little Brown, 1994.

   Surveys the migration, habits, and habitat of a herd of caribou in Alaska.

Van Rose, Susanna. *Volcano & Earthquake.* N.Y.: Knopf. Dist. by Random House, 1992.

   Photos and text explain the causes and effects of volcanoes and earthquakes, and examine specific occurrences throughout history.

Walker, Sally M. *Glaciers: Ice on the Move.* Minneapolis, Minn: Carolrhoda Books, 1990.

   Looks at the formation and movement of different types of glaciers, their effects on the land, and how scientists study glaciers.

PART 2

Alaska's People in Motion

Ice Family

The people of Utqiagvik (today known as Barrow) were used to storms.

These Inupiaq villagers lived in sod houses built over frames of driftwood to keep them snug against such storms. The houses sat back on a bluff overlooking the Arctic Ocean.

On this winter night, a wild storm raged on the small village. Water currents and wind pushed ocean ice chunks against the ice on shore. The chunks broke into great slabs, grinding and tumbling against each other, riding above the bluff. Sometimes the force hurtled heavy blocks high toward the village.

In one house near the bluff, a teenage boy, two young girls, and two older women slept. They had prepared for the storm and were ready to wait it out in comfort.

Suddenly in the black outside, the storm surged against the piles of ice on shore. Huge blocks broke loose and burst over the bluff. The slabs hurtled down on the sod house, burying it and the people inside under tons of ice. Death was quick and quiet.

UTQIAGVIK ARCHAEOLOGY PROJECT

At Utqiagvik, sea ice pushed over the top of a bluff and covered an ancient sod house. Today scientists study the preserved remains to learn how early people lived.

Naluqataq, the blanket toss, in Barrow.
NORTH SLOPE BOROUGH SCHOOL DISTRICT

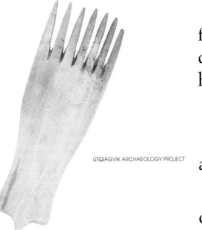

UTQIAGVIK ARCHAEOLOGY PROJECT

By morning most of the house lay hidden and frozen under the ice covering it. Neighbors checking later found the lifeless and crushed house, and left it in peace.

So it stayed for 500 years.

Today, only mounded earth remains where abandoned Utqiagvik houses sat in the past.

In the early 1980s, Barrow leaders considered doing construction in the area. They asked scientists to dig first. The leaders wanted to preserve the artifacts and history of the hidden houses. When human remains came to light, the place was sealed off to digging.

Finally special permission was received from Barrow leaders. With great care, scientists uncovered the ancient family preserved for all those years. Experts learned about the family and their lifestyle.

UTQIAGVIK ARCHAEOLOGY PROJECT

Digging at ancient sites is delicate, time-consuming work.

Scientists found how people of those years built their houses. They found a children's pin-and-ball game made from seal bone. They found ivory combs, tools, weapons, and so much more.

Findings such as those gave clues to the mystery of how early people came to Alaska, and how they lived.

1   The First Alaskans

Scientists are still learning about how plants, animals, and mankind developed from the very beginning on earth. There is evidence through ancient artifacts of people living in northeast Asia thousands of years ago.

Families in Asia roamed in groups then, following the animals for food. In colder lands, a young girl or boy of that time wore skin clothing sewed together with bone needles. Perhaps they lived in tents framed with mastodon bones. Their food was whatever they found—seeds, berries, meat, and fish. Sabre-toothed tigers, mammoths, and giant beavers roamed the land.

During the last great Ice Age about 20,000 years ago, the ocean level lowered. It took a long time, but as the water went down, the Bering Land Bridge became exposed. Over many years, animals traveled over this land bridge into Alaska. Hungry hunters were close behind.

Some of these roaming families made their way through an ice-free passage into North and South America. Many ancient families remained in the North.

Eskimo, Aleut, and Indian people survived in Alaska for centuries before people began writing down history. There was no state called "Alaska" at that time. There were no maps to

USDA FOREST SERVICE, SITKA

Scientists are studying ancient sites in many parts of Alaska. These students from Mt. Edgecumbe High School worked with Forest Service archaeologists near Sitka. They were exploring a Tlingit subsistence site about 800 to 1,000 years old.

Alaska's People in Motion

A Timeline of History

JIM FOWLER

study, no books to read. The first people knew Alaska through their own eyes and in stories passed down from one generation to the next.

These earliest peoples settled mostly where they could find food. Rivers held lots of fish, so some people stayed near the rivers. People found that seal and whale meat fed them and that seal skins made warm clothing. Therefore, some families stayed near the ocean. Other people moved inland and followed the caribou over the tundra.

BERT NEIMEYER

When people live by subsistence, everyone has jobs to do.

Alaska's People in Motion

People cross from Asia to North America over the Bering Land Bridge (10-20,000 years ago)

Russian traders and businessmen come in search of furs (1741-1867)

The United States purchases Alaska (1867)

Alaska's salmon industry begins (1878-1930s)

People rush North for gold (1898-1917)

The U. S. builds the Alaska-Canada Military Highway and strategic military bases (1941-today)

Alaska becomes the 49th State (1959)

Oil on the North Slope prompts the Alaska Native Claims Settlement Act and the TransAlaska Pipeline (1970s)

Alaskans and visitors enjoy "The Great Land" (Today!)

Early Trade Routes

Long before Russians, Europeans, and other Americans came to Alaska, Native people traded among themselves. People from the coast traded seal oil, ivory, and shells for the meat and skins of land animals. Some traded beautiful woven hats, carved ivory, and decorated clothing. Sometimes iron from distant shipwrecks was carried along the trade routes.

Eskimo
Athabaskan
Aleut
Tlingit

Source: Patricia Partnow

Alaska Native traditions are very important to people today. These Tlingit children and their elders wore traditional clothing at Celebration '94 in Juneau.

SEALASKA CORP., MARK KELLEY

Native families lived a *subsistence* life. That means they hunted, trapped, fished, and gathered from land and sea. Their food, tools, shelters, transportation, clothing, toys—everything—came from the *environment*. Villagers worked together and shared the results of their labors.

People especially had a deep respect for the animals they killed. Meat was treated carefully, and there was a use for every part. Very little was wasted.

Early people thought of themselves as one with nature, too. Sometimes men and women talked to the spirits in the animals. They believed if they showed respect and appreciation, there would always be animals to hunt.

Origin of Land and People

In the beginning there was water all over the earth, and it was very cold; the water was covered with ice, and there were no people. Then the ice ground together, making long ridges and hummocks. At this time came a man from the far side of the great water and stopped on the ice hills near where Pikmiktalik now is, taking for his wife a she-wolf. Bye and bye he had many children, which were always born in pairs—a boy and a girl. Each pair spoke a tongue of their own, differing from that of their parents and different from any spoken by any of their brothers or sisters.

As soon as they were large enough each pair was sent out in a different direction from the others, and thus the family spread far and near from the ice hills, which now became snow-covered mountains. As the snow melted it ran down the hillsides, scooping out ravines and river beds, and so making the earth with its streams.

The twins peopled the earth with their children, and as each pair with their children spoke a language different from the others, the various tongues found on earth were established and continue to this day.

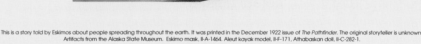

This is a story told by Eskimos about people spreading throughout the earth. It was printed in the December 1922 issue of *The Pathfinder*. The original storyteller is unknown. Artifacts from the Alaska State Museum. Eskimo mask, II-A-1464. Aleut kayak model, II-F-171. Athabaskan doll, II-C-282-1.

Over thousands of years, Native groups settled in many parts of Alaska. Each group existed in ways suited to the land and climate where they lived. Sometimes they traded with each other. Sometimes they fought wars. The *cultures* they passed down are still important to all the people who live in Alaska today.

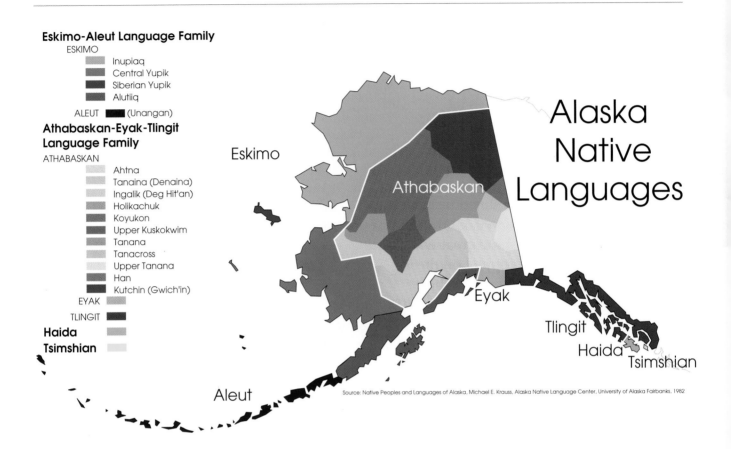

Eskimo-Aleut Language Family

ESKIMO
- Inupiaq
- Central Yupik
- Siberian Yupik
- Alutiiq

ALEUT (Unangan)

Athabaskan-Eyak-Tlingit Language Family

ATHABASKAN
- Ahtna
- Tanaina (Denaina)
- Ingalik (Deg Hit'an)
- Holikachuk
- Koyukon
- Upper Kuskokwim
- Tanana
- Tanacross
- Upper Tanana
- Han
- Kutchin (Gwich'in)

EYAK

TLINGIT

Haida

Tsimshian

Alaska Native Languages

Eskimo

Athabaskan

Eyak

Tlingit

Haida

Tsimshian

Aleut

Source: Native Peoples and Languages of Alaska, Michael E. Krauss, Alaska Native Language Center, University of Alaska Fairbanks. 1982

The 20 Alaska Native languages can be grouped into "families" of languages that are related. Languages within a family are similar to each other. Groups of people within language families, however, may have very different cultures.

2   Yupik and Inupiaq Eskimos

Early Inupiaq and Yupik peoples settled in tundra and forest areas of northern and western Alaska. They learned to live where ice and cold locked the land and waters for much of the year. Some also lived in southwestern Alaska. There the weather was a little kinder. It was wetter and warmer.

In northern Alaska, Inupiaq boys still learn the skills of fishing, hunting, and gathering that are important to subsistence living.

PETER METCALFE

Some families lived along the flat tundra coast. The ocean was their highway, and it supplied their food and everyday needs. Whales, seals, and walruses were their basic food, but they fished, too. It was a great honor for a young boy to be included in his first seal hunt. When he got his first seal, it was the custom to distribute it among the elders. That custom is still followed today.

Other Yupik and Inupiaq families lived inland, hunting on the tundra and in the boreal forests. They fished along the rivers, or hunted caribou or moose. To round out the menu, people gathered bird eggs, berries, and roots. They traveled by boat, or by walking long distances.

Contrary to many stories, Eskimo families did not live in "igloos" or snow houses. Snow houses were built for temporary shelter on winter hunting trips, much as people use tents today. Instead the people built sod houses partly underground to escape the cold.

Seal oil lamps gave heat and light to their homes. In summer, people often moved to outdoor camps.

Knife Stories

Alaska State Museum, II-A-4640

Eskimo women and girls in western Alaska used to tell stories while drawing with story-knives. A storyteller's "paper" was snow, mud, or dirt. Her "pencil" was a carved wooden or ivory knife. She squatted on the ground, drawing a picture as she talked or sang. She'd draw, wipe away that picture, and draw another. Telling stories this way was not only fun, but it passed on history. It also taught people how they should act.

Nowadays storyknifing is not as popular as it used to be. However, some women, girls, and boys still carry on the custom. Sometimes instead of traditional ivory or wooden knives, storytellers use butter knives or flattened spoons.

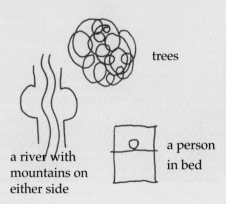

trees

a river with mountains on either side

a person in bed

NANCY RABENER

Sharing and working together are an important part of the subsistence lifestyle. These people are picking salmon from a set net at Woolley Lagoon near Nome.

These people are working together on St. Lawrence Island.

DOUGLAS YATES

Everyone in the family had jobs to do. Men braved the weather to hunt or fish. They made tools and boats for living or hunting. Women took care of the game once it was caught. They cooked and preserved it. They sewed skins for clothing. Women also gathered plants, roots, and berries. Boys and girls learned these skills by watching their parents and helping with the work.

Life was not all work. People held dances, sang songs, and played games. They had times of happiness and times of sadness as we do today. Like early people everywhere, they told about their life through stories.

To the Eskimos, as to people all over the world, stories helped to explain the world around them. Some kinds of stories taught people how to live together. For instance, take this Point Barrow Inupiaq tale about the ten-legged polar bear. The story tells of sharing, and goes something like this:

In a village there were two houses side by side. In the first lived a family with children. The second house had many people who were related. One winter people in the second house got a walrus. Even though there was not much food then, the people did not share the meat.

The next day the father in the first house went out to hunt seals. His family was very hungry. He stumbled upon the den of the huge ten-legged polar bear. After outwitting the bear and fighting with it, the man killed it. He took one of the legs back to his house to eat. The next day he cut up the bear. Though people in the second house had not shared the walrus, the father in the first house shared bear with them anyway.

This story came from Northern Tales, selected and edited by Howard Norman.

Through stories such as this, children learned how they were expected to live.

Sharing has always been an important part of Native life. Each hunter did not find game every day. It took many people to catch and bring home a whale or walrus. Families depended on one another.

In those days, people counted time by seasons and what was happening around them. Here is an example of how some Yupik people named the months:

LYDIA APATIKI

Joshua Apatiki of Gambell, on St. Lawrence Island, is wearing a parka made of bird skins, pants made of reindeer fawn, and boots of sealskin. His clothing was made by his grandmother, Lydia Apatiki, in the traditional Siberian Yupik way. In the background are traditional walrus skin boats.

English	Yupik	What it means
January	*Iralull'er*	the bad month
February	*Kanruyauciq*	frost
March	*Kepnerciq*	cutting time
April	*Tengmiirvik*	geese come
May	*Kayangut Anutiit*	coming of eggs
June	*Kaugun*	hitting (of fish)
July	*Ingun*	molting (of birds)
August	*Tengun*	flight (of birds)
September	*Amirairvik*	(caribou) shed velvet
October	*Qaariitaarvik*	masked festivals
November	*Cauyarvik*	time of drumming
December	*Uivik*	time of going around

From Steven A. Jacobson, Yup'ik Eskimo Dictionary, Alaska Native Language Center, 1984.

NANCY RABENER

For people living close to the land, life depends on knowing the seasons.

ALASKA STATE LIBRARY, EARLY PRINTS OF ALASKA COLLECTION

3 · Aleuts and Alutiiqs

Most early Aleut families lived on the long string of islands in southwestern Alaska that we now call the Aleutian Chain.

Since the Aleutian Islands are distant from the mainland, there are few land animals there. Aleut hunters, then, took to the sea.

Harsh weather ruled the Aleutians. Wind could be a monster, sometimes whipping up to 140 miles an hour. That's worse than a hurricane! It was often foggy and stormy there, too. But the ocean never froze, as it did further north.

In spite of heavy fog most of the time, hunters bravely took off in small skin-covered canoes called *kayaks* to hunt sea lions, seals, sea otters, and whales. The hunters were skilled in locating land even when they could not see it through the fog.

Sometimes early Aleut people lived in small villages of maybe six or seven houses. Up to 20 people might share a building that was entered through the roof. Each village had its own hunting area.

Aleut and Alutiiq people lived close to the sea.

AMNWR, ED BAILEY

Aleut women were known for making delicate and beautiful grass baskets. They grew their fingernails long especially for shredding blades of grass to weave the baskets. Only a few people know how to make these baskets today.

Early Native people expressed themselves through pictures.

Not too long ago, people exploring some caves found *pictographs*, or ancient paintings. These were possibly made by Alutiiq people who lived on the Alaska Peninsula, on Kodiak Island, and along Prince William Sound. Think about how these paintings might have come about.

ALASKA DIVISION OF TOURISM, ERNEST SCHNEIDER

A few people today know how to make traditional Aleut baskets. Some baskets are woven so fine they can hold water.

Imagine you are one of several men returning from a hunt on the ocean. Paddling along in your skin kayaks, you are still far from home. You see a storm coming up. Quickly you look for a piece of beach where you can drag your skin kayaks ashore. Nearby is a river, and driftwood is washed up along the shore. You see what looks like a cave with an overhanging rock. A shelter. You just make shore before the raging storm strikes.

Together you build a fire in the cave. While your friends tell stories, you powder a red stone from the beach and mix the dust with seal oil and water. You pound the end of a spruce root for a brush, then dip it into the paste. In the flickering light from the fire, you paint a "jumping" whale on the rock wall close by.

This pictograph of a deer, found in southcentral Alaska, may be as much as 500 years old.

Copied from a reproduction by Buck Hayden in *The Alaska Journal*. Reproduced with permission of Alaska Northwest Publishing Co.

ALASKA STATE MUSEUM

Nowadays Aleut people proudly share their traditional culture. One man taught a workshop on how to make bentwood hats.

The Athabaskan Indians make good use of the birch trees that grow throughout interior Alaska. Here a woman makes a traditional basket of birch bark in the village of Minto, northwest of Fairbanks.

A painting like this was found by people hundreds of years later. It is a lasting memory.

Besides their culture from the past, Aleuts gave something else to the future. The Aleut language gave Alaska its name. "Alaxsxa" is the original Aleut name for "Alaska." Alaxsxa means "mainland," or "the object toward which the action of the sea is directed." Over the years since early use, the word has become "Alaska"—The Great Land.

4 Athabaskan and Eyak Indians

Most Athabaskan Indian groups settled in the boreal forests of central Alaska. They trapped fur animals and hunted caribou, moose, rabbits, and beaver. They fished along the mighty rivers, or along the Gulf of Alaska.

Some people moved about often, looking for food. They carried their houses of caribou or moose skins with them. Others settled in permanent villages.

Athabaskans from different parts of central Alaska spoke different languages. Only groups living close to each other could understand each other. Today there are still 11 different Athabaskan languages spoken in Alaska.

Athabaskans, like other Native people, did not try to rule nature. They tried to live in harmony with it. For instance, they had a close bond with

ALASKA DIVISION OF TOURISM, ERNEST SCHNEIDER
Basket, ALASKA STATE MUSEUM, II-C-21

the animals they hunted. They believed animals had power. People still believe that today.

Alaskan author Richard Nelson wrote about what one Koyukon Athabaskan man told him:

Some old timers—Chief John, Old Thomas, Big John— told me this a long time ago: Every hair on a brown bear's hide has a life of its own. Every hair moves, vibrates by itself when something surprises the bear; so it can't keep still, it can't keep its temper. It takes a few years for all that life to be gone from a brown bear's hide. That's the kind of power it has.

This story is from Richard Nelson, Make Prayers to the Raven.

Like their Yupik and Inupiaq neighbors, the early Athabaskans traveled by boat or on foot. In winter it was easier to travel along frozen rivers and lakes.

Over land, however, deep snows made walking hard. How did Native peoples master this problem? By inventing a certain kind of "shoe."

Indians in interior Alaska survived the deep snows by making snowshoes from birch wood and animal rawhide. Snowshoes acted like a stiff net on top of the snow to keep the person wearing them from sinking down. Without them, a hunter could get stuck in waist high snow. He might not be able to move fast enough to keep from freezing.

If a snowshoe broke on the trail, a traveler had to make another one, right then. That was done by bending a frame of green willow wood,

Traditional Athabaskan Uses of White Spruce

OUTER BARK

Roofing and flooring
Dye

INNER BARK

Medicinal tea
Bandages

SAP

Medicinal use

NEEDLES

Medicinal tea

DEAD WOOD

Firewood
Tanning Smoke

TRUNK

Logs and planks
Firewood
Rafts
Tent Frames

PITCH

Advesive
Waterproofing
Chewing gum

CONES

Cone dust:
drys up
runny ears

ROOTS

Lashing
Eye medicine
Tea

From *Make Prayers to the Raven* by Richard Nelson.

PAT STANLEY

Author Velma Wallis of Fort Yukon inspired people all over the world with her book *Two Old Women,* a legend of the Gwich'in people. She is shown here with her mother and daughter.

The Naa Kahidi Theater dramatized stories of Alaska's Native people for audiences in the United States, Canada, and Europe. Here they enact the legend "How Raven Brought Water to the World."

MARTY SOHL

then weaving bark strips across it. This emergency snowshoe worked well enough to get the person home safely.

Like children of many lands, Indian children growing up in those times had jobs to do for the family. Boys and girls were expected to learn by watching and copying adults. Sometimes adults told stories to teach children how to behave. Here is a legend told by the Eyaks, people who lived on the shores of Prince William Sound. It is called "Taking Away by Owl" and was told by Galushia Nelson.

Once there was a very bad boy at one of the villages who was crying for this and that. No matter what you gave him he would want something else and would cry until he gets it. One of the wise men used to tell his mother that Owl will get him if he does not stop crying for everything. But he was hard to please, and one night an Owl did come down through the smoke hole on top of the house and take him away and was never seen again.

This story is from *Eyak Legends of the Copper River Delta,* compiled by John F.C. Johnson.

It was not hard for boys and girls to know what lesson this story taught.

5   Tlingit, Haida, and Tsimshian Indians

The Tlingit Indians settled in southeastern Alaska. Theirs was a warmer, wetter climate.

The coastal rainforest of southeastern Alaska was especially important to the Tlingits. From its tall trees, using stone tools, they carved canoes, house poles, and objects for ceremonies and everyday use. Totem poles as we know them today did not become common until after explorers landed in Alaska. It was then most metal tools were available.

Tlingits also built large houses of wood planks in which as many as 12 families lived. They used roots and bark from spruce and cedar trees to make clothing and baskets.

Families and family relations were very important. Each Tlingit person belonged to a clan within one of two large groups. They were either Ravens or Eagles. Each clan had its own hunting areas, dances, songs, and designs for art. Many of these customs have continued to present years.

The Tlingits lived from the sea and rivers. They fished for salmon and halibut. They gathered clams, herring eggs, and seaweed from the beaches.

Salmon was the most important fish. It was the main food, and the Indians respected it greatly.

The importance of fish carried over into one of the children's pastimes. The game was "fish trap." One child was "the fish," while the others were "the fishermen." The fish person was allowed a head start, and dashed away. Then the fishermen grabbed each others' hands to form a net. They would run wildly after the fish to catch it. It was a lot like games children play today.

ALASKA STATE MUSEUM, V-A-339

Theodore J. Richardson's watercolor of Wrangell shows Tlingit houses in about 1890.

Living by the Seasons

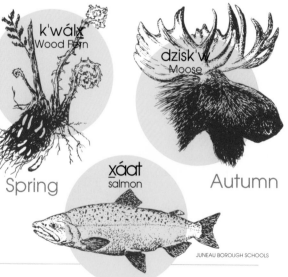

k'wálx
Wood Fern

dzisk'w
Moose

xáat
salmon

Spring

Autumn

Summer

JUNEAU BOROUGH SCHOOLS

ALASKA STATE MUSEUM II-B-811

This Haida hat was made of split spruce root and is decorated with a Raven design.

Haida Indians did not live in Alaska during those very early years. A group of Haidas moved north into Alaska from the Queen Charlotte Islands in Canada about 1775. They settled on Prince of Wales Island, at the southern tip of Alaska.

The Haidas were much admired for carving great cedar canoes, sometimes 70 feet long. That's about as long as six pickup trucks lined up end to end. Carving was all done by cutting from one single tree. Every inch!

Tsimshian Indians, too, did not come to Alaska until later. A small group of Tsimshians moved north from Canada. They arrived in 1887, led by a churchman, Father William Duncan (1832-1918). The group came to build a model community at Metlakatla, on an island near where the town of Ketchikan is today.

Early Metlakatla was known for its neat picket fences and wooden sidewalks.

For several thousand years, Eskimos, Aleuts, and Indians lived in Alaska. No one counted them, but people who study history estimate there were about 60,000 Native people then. Today, nearly 90,000 Native people live in Alaska, but more than 500,000 other people do, too.

Where did these other Alaskans come from? And why?

BENJAMIN A. HALDANE, ALASKA STATE LIBRARY, D. REPLOGLE COLLECTION

6 Russian Explorers Enter the New World

Some people are always curious.

Beginning 500 or 600 years ago, and even before that, explorers from Europe sailed west trying to reach the riches of China and India. They didn't realize North America was in the way, and they kept bumping into it. As a result of those journeys, people came to America and settled what is now the Lower 48 states.

ALASKA STATE LIBRARY, ALASKA CENTENNIAL COLLECTION

Early ships that visited Alaska almost always carried artists, who recorded the scenes that they saw.

Explorers from Russia, however, grew curious about what land was **east**. A few sailors had landed on Alaskan soil and brought back stories about a "big country" out there. Alaska had no name then. It was simply "a lot of land." Just before he died, Russia's Czar Peter the Great (1672-1725) sent the Danish sea captain Vitus Bering to find out what that land was really like.

Vitus Bering (1681-1741) sailed twice to Alaska. The last time, in 1741, he landed on Kayak Island in the Gulf of Alaska. Although Bering died on the return trip to Russia, his sailors brought back hundreds of sea otter pelts. Chinese merchants wanted the fur for coats, and they paid fabulous prices for the pelts. Once Russian traders and adventurers saw the pelts, they began sailing to Alaska to get more.

For the next 40 or 50 years, traders, merchants, and sea captains from Russia made fabulous money gathering sea otter furs from around Alaska. Sometimes Aleut and Alutiiq hunters helped them, and the people worked together. Sometimes the newcomers forced the Natives to hunt and were very cruel to them.

The czar allowed a company of businessmen to establish a Russian settlement at Kodiak in 1784. By 1799 a business called the Russian-American Company was put in charge of work there. The settlement was headed by Alexander Baranof (1747-1819), who was made governor of Russian America. The company's headquarters later moved to New Archangel, the town later named Sitka.

Along with company workers came storekeepers, Russian church people, and a few families. This was about the same time in history that the capital of the United States was moved from Philadelphia to Washington, D.C.

The late 1700s also brought explorers from other countries. Englishman James Cook (1728-1779) was the first European to step on Alaska's northwest coast. Another Englishman, George Vancouver (1757-1798) came later. Spanish explorers made visits to villages along Alaska's southern coast. The city of Cordova is named for a Spanish explorer who visited the area in 1790.

ALASKA STATE LIBRARY

The first explorers did not know much about Alaska. This early map showed much more about Russia than about the New World.

The French, too, sailed north to explore. So did the Americans. Many times the explorers met Natives and Russians who had arrived there before them.

Even though the Russian fur company had settled in New Archangel, Governor Baranof had to fight to stay. The Tlingit Indians near Sitka did not like the Russians there.

At last a shaky agreement was made. The Russians stayed in New Archangel, and they did trade with the Indians. Not until 1867, when the United States bought Alaska, did the Russians officially leave.

Although the Russians departed, they left some of their culture in Alaska. Some Russians married Native people, and their family lines continue today. While they governed, the Russians brought schools and their religion to

STEVE KESSLER

St. Michael's Cathedral in Sitka is a reminder of Russian influence in Alaska.

Math Challenge

Sea Otter

Russian and Chinese people valued sea otter fur for its softness. They called it "soft gold." The fur blocked ocean water from getting through to the animal's skin, and kept it warm

Sea otter fur is special because it is so dense, or packed together. There are about one million (1,000,000) hairs per **square inch** in a sea otter's pelt. That's one inch! On the average human's **whole head** there are only about 100,000 hairs.

Imagine taking the hairs from one square inch of sea otter fur. (That's 1,000,000 hairs.) Now suppose you put them on human heads at the normal thickness of human hair. (That's 100,000 hairs on each human head.)

How many human heads would a square inch of sea otter fur cover?

ALASKA DIVISION OF TOURISM, ROBERT ANGELL

J. PENNELOPE GOFORTH

Alaska's Russian heritage can be seen in the Russian Orthodox churches people attend in many Alaska towns and villages. This church in Unalaska is the oldest in the state.

many Natives. Today there are Russian Orthodox churches in Alaska. Alaskans recognize the double-headed eagle emblem. Russian names for streets, people, and places are found in different parts of the state.

However, the coming of Russians and other explorers to Alaska was harmful in some ways. Outsiders brought new germs that Native people were not used to. The germs caused flu, smallpox, measles, and other diseases that killed thousands of Native people.

Russian doctors tried to vaccinate the people to protect them from smallpox. But many Natives did not trust the newcomers and would not take the vaccinations.

Results of the diseases on Native families were crushing. Sometimes whole villages of people died overnight. Children were left without parents. Older people were abandoned. Few men were left to hunt and provide food for the village.

Nobody knows for sure how many people lived in Alaska after the Russians came. But experts who study history think the population of Alaska was down by thousands of people. When the Russians sold Alaska to the United States, there were about 28,000 people living in the Great Land.

Some Early Russian Settlements
(1741–1867)

Most early Russian settlements were along the coast of Alaska or on the Yukon River. The Russians stayed mostly in areas where they could find furs of sea otters, land otters, and fur seals.

Nulato
Unalakleet
St. Michael
Russian Mission
Kasilof
Kenai
Seward
Yakutat
Nushagak
Wrangell
Sitka
St. Paul
St. George
Kodiak
Attu
Unalaska
Atka

Source: K. H. Stone, "Some Geographic Bases for Planning New Alaskan Settlement," Science in Alaska, 1950.

7 Whale Hunters Move North

Even though Native peoples had been whaling and living in Alaska for thousands of years, the Russians claimed Alaska and the seas around it as theirs. The Russians did not like other newcomers in their waters. However, they had war and other problems in their own country. They did not have the men and ships to keep other newcomers out.

ALASKA STATE MUSEUM, II-A-5852

Scrimshaw shows a whaling expedition on an ivory whale tooth from King Island.

During the middle 1800s, American whale hunters came to the coasts of California and Alaska looking for whales. The world did not have electricity then. Great quantities of whale oil were burned in lamps for light in buildings.

Years later, coal, gas, and then electricity replaced whale oil for lighting. After that, the hunt for whales slowed down.

Whaling by non-Native people also lessened in the 1860s, partly because Americans were fighting the Civil War in the United States.

Outsiders came to Alaskan waters to capture large numbers of whales. Besides whale oil they were after **baleen,** the huge, hanging plates some kinds of whales have instead of teeth. In the photo below, the baleen is the brush-like material you can see along the roof of the whale's mouth.

ALASKA STATE LIBRARY, EARLY PRINTS COLLECTION

Not many new people moved to Alaska because of whaling. The ships came for only a few months in the summer. Whalers did meet and trade with Inupiaq-speaking people in the Arctic. They established some whaling bases on shore. When the whalers left the North, they carried

81

information and maps about Alaska to people who lived in other places.

Native people along Alaska's northern and western coasts continue their long tradition of whaling even today. The Alaska Eskimo Whaling Commission helps to create world agreements to make sure not too many whales are killed.

8   The United States Buys Alaska

Whether the Russians owned Alaska or not, they sold it to the Americans for $7.2 million. Alaska became a U. S. Territory on March 30, 1867. The official change of flags took place at Sitka later that year.

With this check the United States purchased Alaska from Russia. The total cost was $7.2 million, or less than two cents per acre.

Many everyday people of the United States thought it was foolish to buy a cold, frozen land like Alaska. On the other hand, reports from northern fishermen, miners, whalers, and traders had made their way back to Congress. Lawmakers in Washington, D.C., probably knew Alaska was a good buy.

Even at that, the U.S. government did not know what to do with Alaska. The Territory was so isolated that no one really knew what laws would work there.

Some people thought Alaska might be a good place for a jail. Just ship all lawbreakers there, they said, the way England shipped its convicts to Australia a little earlier in the century. Luckily that was just a passing idea.

Still, a number of Americans grew curious about Alaska. Some thought they might be able to come here to make a new start, or to find gold. Already a few Americans searched for gold in southeastern Alaska, while up north, merchants steamed up and down the Yukon River setting up stores and trading with people along the route.

ALASKA DIVISION OF TOURISM

Steam-powered riverboats called *sternwheelers* carried people and freight along Alaska rivers in early days. The sternwheeler *Discovery* is a tourist attraction in Fairbanks.

But settling in Alaska was not like settling the West in the United States. You could not ride a covered wagon to Alaska, or take a train. There were no planes then either. Besides, the country of Canada was between the United States and Alaska.

Canada was owned by England, and it had its own rules and government. The Canadian land between the U.S. and Alaska was wild with mountains and rivers and forests. People did hike there, but walking was hard going.

Revenue cutters were sent North to enforce law and order, but they ended up doing many other things as well.

Instead of going by land, then, people used the ocean as their highway. After the purchase of Alaska, the U.S. government sent ships called "revenue cutters" to the north. These lightly armed boats were part of the U.S. Revenue Service (now the Coast Guard). The cutters stopped at Alaska villages along the coast.

ALASKA STATE LIBRARY, U.S. REVENUE CUTTER SVC. COLLECT

U.S.COAST GUARD, DON ATWELL

Nowadays the U.S. Coast Guard maintains nearly 1,300 aids to navigation in Alaska. That includes lighthouses and buoys like the one, above, being worked on by the buoy tender *Elderberry*.

Alaska's first salmon cannery opened in Klawock in 1878.

KEITH STIGEN

Through the early years of the Territory, cutters did everything. They were courtrooms, jails, hospitals, dental offices, schools, and churches. They were like floating communities.

When the U.S. bought Alaska, it did not realize it had doubled its coastline! Not all of the Alaska coast had been mapped. The cutters later brought scientists who began charting every bay and island. In 1902 the first lighthouse was built. Good maps and water aids made travel safer for all ships.

However, while the government was arranging water safety aids, and preparing to chart the Alaska coastline, more ships arrived. They were the fishermen, in search of another of Alaska's riches—salmon.

9   The Fish Cannery Connection

Salmon fishing, like whaling, did not start on a special date. Fish have been a basic food for families since the beginning of history.

You already know the coastline of Alaska is long. You know fish like cold water. You know a great portion of offshore Alaska land is continental shelf. Therefore, you have to know there are a lot of fish and shellfish out there.

Alaskan Indians, Eskimos, and Aleuts had known that through history. Once other people arrived and explored, it did not take them long to figure that out, too. In the late 1800s some Americans decided that money could be made

84

The Tlingits have a myth of "How the Fish Came Into the Sea."
This story was told by Billy Wilson Senior of Hoonah in 1974.
The legend not only tells how the fish came into the world.
It also tells the order of their migration.

How the Fish Came Into the Sea

After Raven bring daylight to all the people he keep walkin' north, lookin' around, he keep going up, up north. And he see something big, big just like a scow way out on the sea, like a floating box, and he ask:

'What is it out there?'

'That's a tank. All different kinds of fish in there. They try to keep them in there so there's no fish going around this ocean.'

Well, he's thinkin' about it, how he's gonna get it.

Raven send that black and white bird with the long tail—the magpie—to go up and cut a can for him, and he fix it like octopus finger, he carve it like two tentacles of the octopus. He's gonna try to drag in that big scow with it, no matter how far off a thing is, that octopus finger can will always reach it.

In the evening Raven got all the peoples together and they beat drums. He hold the can in his hands and move it around, going up, going down, going around, testing it.

All right. That woman said she's satisfied with it. Then he get all the peoples down on the beach and they begin to sing, and he start to hook it, he tried to pull that thing ashore. And he tried again.

'OOOH, OOOH, OOOH, OH, OH!'

Saying to the people 'Sing stronger all the time' and he tried again.

And he begin to draw it in to shore little by little. Finally he pull it onto the beach and he jump inside, and he open each door. He open the doors for smelts (fish, small fish) and the smelts comes out from that tank. After that herrings, and oolichons, and out of the other sides, king salmon first, and humpies, and coho, and later on the one they call the fall fish, dog salmon, and last comes the ones that stop, the halibut and flounders and cod, and he pushed them out.

See, just the way he opened the doors, is just the way they come every year. No mistake on it. And Raven is satisfied, he released all that fish to go around this world.

From the Tlingit myth "How the Fish Came Into the Sea," as told to Billy Wilson Senior from *Indian Fishing* by Hilary Stewart ©1977.
Original recording and transcript by kind permission of Paul Bragstad. Published by Douglas & McIntyre. Reprinted by permission.

Courtesy ROBERT N. OSBORNE

by canning Alaska fish and selling it around the world. Salmon canneries sprang up in southeastern Alaska first, then in Kodiak, and later near Bristol Bay.

Everyone knew that when salmon spawned, they migrated from the ocean back to the rivers, streams, and lakes where they were hatched. In those years, traps were built across the mouths of rivers, with canneries close by. The fish **had** to go that way to get upstream and spawn. Not many fish escaped the traps. As years went by, there were fewer and fewer fish.

Another problem arose in the cannery industry. After a cannery was built, an owner might not allow Natives to fish on cannery property, even though they had been fishing on that river for centuries. On the other hand, some cannery owners hired Natives, which gave work to people nearby.

Although the canning industry grew until the 1930s, it did not bring very many people to live in Alaska. Cannery owners and most fishermen lived in other places. They just came to Alaska to fish during the season.

Sometimes cannery owners brought in Chinese people who would work for low wages. But almost everyone left after the canning season. In the 1920s many Filipino workers called "Alaskeros" came to Alaska to work in canneries. A number of their descendants live here today.

ALASKA SEAFOOD MARKETING INSTITUTE

Processing Alaska's seafood still provides jobs for many Alaskans and seasonal workers.

Some of the people who came to support the salmon industry did stay to live in Alaska. They were storekeepers, dock workers, government people, and their families. That was enough to help towns such as Cordova, Dillingham, and Ketchikan grow.

10 A Rush North for Gold

As you have seen, not many of the newcomers who came to harvest Alaska's fur, whales, and fish settled in the Territory. What, then, **did** bring people north to stay? It was not what was in the oceans, but what was under the ground.

Stories of finding gold in Alaska had traveled south for many years. Gold was found in the Canadian Cassiar district, near the Stikine River, in the 1870s. Later, in 1880, gold was found near what is now Juneau in southeastern Alaska. There were other gold discoveries, too.

But the big strike came in 1896, and it was not even in Alaska! It was in an area along the Yukon River in Canada, with the focus on Dawson City. The strike caused the Klondike Gold Rush of 1898. Canadian author Pierre Berton wrote a book about the Gold Rush called *The Klondike Fever*. And fever it was. Adventurers went crazy to get to Alaska.

UNIVERSITY OF WASHINGTON LIBRARY, SPECIAL COLLECTIONS, HEGG 1391

In 1898, when the world learned that gold had been found in the Klondike, thousands of people rushed North to make their fortunes. Few realized their dreams, but the great stampede changed Alaska forever.

A few children joined their families in the rush for gold. They often traveled hundreds of miles, suffering cold and other hardships. Sometimes their efforts were rewarded, sometimes not.

ALASKA STATE LIBRARY, WINTER AND POND COLLECTION

News about the gold spread to all corners of the world. The Klondike became a magnet for people who wanted to "strike it rich."

There were many routes to the Klondike. Some of the best routes went up the west coasts of the United States and Canada. Then the routes traveled through Alaska to the Klondike.

Eager to make their fortunes, men and women crowded onto boats in Seattle and San Francisco. Many sailed up the *Inside Passage* through the islands of southeastern Alaska to Skagway.

Some struggled over the Coast Mountains, carrying heavy packs on their backs. Some built boats or sleds to cross lakes. Some tramped hundreds of miles in ice and snow.

Other gold seekers traveled to St. Michael on Alaska's western coast. Then they steamed more than 1,700 miles up the Yukon River through Alaska and Canada to the Klondike.

A Young Stampeder

It was unusual for children to hike over the Chilkoot Trail during the Klondike Gold Rush of 1897. But seven-year-old Vera Barnes did. Here is part of her account, which was written up in a San Francisco newspaper, *The Weekly Examiner*, Sept. 23, 1897:

I would get so cold—ooh, so cold—[she said] that I would have to stamp my feet and slap my hands together to get them warm. I did walk fifteen miles in the day, though—without any dinner, too. That was the day we crossed the summit. The summit is a steep, steep place, with steps cut in, and I slipped once and nearly fell, but one of the men caught me and straightened me up again. It was so high and steep that nobody wanted to look back...

When we got to the top there was a sliding place about as wide as a sack of flour down the other side, and we sat down in that and slid instead of walking.

From there Vera hiked to Tagish Lake where the men built boats. Then she and her family floated by boat down to Dawson City, Canada.

Which Way to the Gold?

CANADA

Up the Yukon River
NOME
ST. MICHAEL
FAIRBANKS
FORTYMILE
DAWSON
Float the Yukon River
Iditarod Trail
Valdez Glacier Trail
Valdez-Richardson Trail
WHITEHORSE
Chilkoot Trail
White Pass Trail
VALDEZ
HAINES
SKAGWAY
JUNEAU
SEWARD
GULF OF ALASKA
Ships from Seattle
Ships from Seattle

There were a number of stampeders who never made it at all.

People flowed to Alaska in great streams. Skagway, a little camp of a few people, swelled to thousands in the late 1890s. Everyone was in a fever to stake a claim. Along with these stampeders came storekeepers, bankers, blacksmiths, and even photographers, who hoped to make their fortunes, too.

There were other gold stampedes after the Klondike. Gold was discovered on the beaches of Nome, Alaska, in 1898.

Though it was far from the Klondike, people rushed to Nome any way they could. Those already in the Klondike headed west. Winter did not stop the stampeders. Sometimes 12 dog teams a day left the town of Eagle on the Yukon River. The trip was 1,500 miles from Eagle to Nome. That's like walking from Seattle to Phoenix, Arizona, with no roads, and through rough, cold wilderness.

ALASKA STATE LIBRARY, W. AND R. HUNT COLLECTION

In 1900, thousands of people rushed to Nome, hoping to find gold on the beaches. Today Nome has fewer people, but it is a center of trade and transportation for surrounding areas.

Rescue in the Far North

—September, 1897

At the same time the Klondike Gold Rush was going on, another drama was happening farther north. In September 1897, eight American whaling ships with 275 men were caught in the winter ice off Point Barrow. There were no airplanes then. Boats and supplies could not get through.

Barrow was a small Inupiaq village then. People there had food just enough for themselves to live through the winter. Outsiders hearing about this disaster felt the whalers would surely starve to death before the winter was over.

The U.S. Revenue Cutter *Bear* brought supplies north as far as Nelson Island in the Bering Sea. There the ship met arctic sea ice.

A small overland relief expedition set off in December. Guided and aided by Natives, collecting and driving reindeer with them, the group struggled through frozen wilderness toward Barrow. That's a distance of 1,600 miles!

Three months later the expedition made Barrow, with fresh meat "on the hoof." The whalers had been kept alive until then by Native people hunting and sharing their food. Without that cooperation, the men surely would have died. As it turned out, not one man lost his life from the ordeal!

The U.S. revenue cutter *Bear* was stopped by sea ice near Nelson Island in 1887.

UNIVERSITY OF ALASKA FAIRBANKS, ALASKA & POLAR REGIONS DEPT., SAMUEL CALL COLLECTION

People were desperate to get to Nome. Frozen rivers were the trails. Many walked the entire distance. Some ice skated. A few took bicycles—at minus 20 degrees!

In 1902 gold was found near the Tanana River in central Alaska. In the years that followed, the town of Fairbanks grew up there, built by hopeful miners and business people.

Alaska was not just gold rich. In the early 1900s, oil and coal were discovered in southcentral Alaska near Katalla. A few years later, copper was found in the Wrangell Mountains, and the town of Kennicott was built.

Although Eskimos and Indians often led men to gold claims in the first place, the laws of that time did not allow Natives to share in the profits. Neither could women. To most Natives, the stampeders were mainly obstacles to their hunting.

Some Natives earned money, however, cutting wood for the steamboats. Others traded furs or bought goods at the stores and trading posts that sprang up. Several Native villages even moved from along smaller rivers to the banks of the Yukon. There work and trade goods were close at hand.

STEVE KESSLER

Small mines are still active along the Taylor Highway in Alaska's Fortymile district.

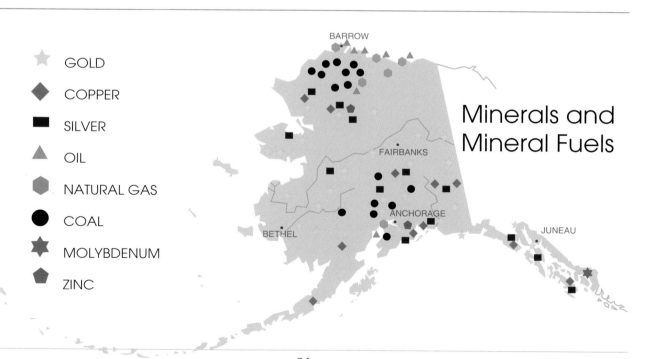

★ GOLD

◆ COPPER

■ SILVER

▲ OIL

⬡ NATURAL GAS

● COAL

✦ MOLYBDENUM

⬠ ZINC

BARROW

FAIRBANKS

ANCHORAGE

BETHEL

JUNEAU

Minerals and Mineral Fuels

DAN JACOBSON

Valdez had its beginnings in Gold Rush days. Today it is the port at the end of the TransAlaska pipeline.

A great number of stampeders returned to their homes after the strikes ended. But many newcomers liked Alaska, its people, and the chances for a new life. They stayed. Gold camps such as Nome, Juneau, Fairbanks, Cordova, Seward, and Valdez became towns and cities.

The Alaska Territory grew in those years. Its population, which was 33,000 before the gold rushes, doubled in the years after.

Most of the new people were non-Natives, and most were not used to living off the land. They wanted the foods and clothing they were used to. They wanted mail from their families back home. They wanted to start businesses. They needed schools, churches, libraries, and laws to keep things in order.

In early days, Alaskans delivered the U.S. Mail by whatever means they could find. This sled traveled the Nome-Teller route.

11 Connecting Up

The gold rushes proved to people that they needed better transportation and communication across the vast land of Alaska. How could they receive supplies or mail, send for a doctor, or do business without railroads, roads, phones, or telegraphs? Now Alaskans have satellites, faxes, and computers to send messages, but people didn't have them then.

Stop a minute and think of this. In 1900, it might take a winter letter **three months(!)** to journey from St. Michael in western Alaska to Washington, D.C.

ALASKA STATE LIBRARY, LOMEN BROTHERS

Then it would take another three months for an answer to travel back to St. Michael. Letters might travel by dogteam, small boat, steamer, train, and horse-drawn sleigh. Can you imagine: **six months** for a letter and its answer. That's half a year!

Lawmakers in Washington, D.C. knew they could not govern the new Territory this way. Business could not be conducted efficiently either. So they came up with money to build a telegraph system in Alaska.

By 1904, several coastal cities, including Sitka and Valdez were linked by telegraph cable underwater to Seattle. At last some Alaskans were connected to the rest of the world.

Laying telegraph wire cable overland across Alaska, however, brought special problems. The U.S. Army Signal Corps laid wire over mountains, across rivers, through snow, often in very cold weather. With stops, the soldiers could only put up about two miles of wire a day.

ALASKA STATE LIBRARY, U.S. ARMY SIGNAL CORPS COLLECTION

Early communication systems depended on operators to receive and pass on information.

When the Signal Corps finished, not every home had telephones as we know them today. Then, villages were lucky to have telegraph connections every 25 miles for emergencies. Soon after, land wires were replaced by wireless radio.

The railroad was next. Ships could bring supplies to coastal towns, but they couldn't reach the interior of Alaska easily. A few short railroads were built in the early 1900s. For example, the Copper River and Northwestern was used to bring copper out to ships on the coast. It also provided entrance north to the interior of Alaska.

Comin' Round the Mountain

One early railroad was the White Pass and Yukon. During the Klondike gold rush, stampeders found it hard struggling over the steep mountains to the goldfields. The trail climbed 3,000 feet to the summit and continued into Canada. In summer it was muddy and steep. In winter it was freezing cold and steep. When Canadian and American engineers decided to build a railroad over the Pass, people smiled and shook their heads.

Yet, in the summer of 1898, a narrow gauge railroad was begun from Skagway. It was "narrow" because the rails were only three feet apart as compared to standard rails, which were wider.

It took three years to hack and build a railbed up the mountains. Two thousand men worked at any one time. They truly carved a way with blasting powder. The mountainsides were so steep in spots, the workers had to lower a man by rope to the rock face so he could drill holes for blasting powder. Many men stayed and completed the job. Some took off for the gold fields.

When the White Pass and Yukon Railroad was done in 1900, it traveled 20 miles through Alaska and 90 miles through Canada to Whitehorse in the Yukon Territory. After the gold rush, the trains hauled freight and passengers throughout the year. Today coaches carry tourists to the summit and back during the summer.

Constructing the railroad was such a feat of engineering, the White Pass and Yukon has been named an International Historic Civil Engineering Landmark. That puts it in the same class as the Statue of Liberty and the Panama Canal.

ALASKA DIVISION OF TOURISM

Building railroads in Alaska was not easy. It was hard work to construct tracks over mountains, rivers, and such wild country. Often permafrost added to the problems. The cost was tremendously high.

One central Alaska railroad was built, nevertheless. What would later become the Alaska Railroad began in Seward and ran north. A construction camp was built on the shore of Cook Inlet. This camp grew into the town of Anchorage. Several years later, in 1923, the railroad ran all the way to Fairbanks.

ALASKA DIVISION OF TOURISM

Nowadays, high technology such as satellites and this microwave station connect Alaskans with each other and the world. People communicate by telephone, fax, television, and computer.

12 Alaskans Take to the Air

Still, Alaska's size and rugged landscape made connections difficult. It was the airplane that really made the difference in the Territory.

In a vast country of mountains, rivers, and glaciers, the sky above became the needed highway. Even in early days, when airplanes were slow and unreliable, a trip that might take 22 days by dog sled was covered in three hours by plane!

In August of 1920 the first cross-country flight was made from Washington, D.C. to Nome, Alaska. It took almost 54 hours (two days plus) flying time, covering 4,500 miles, at what was then a smashing 115 miles an hour. One of the pilots said later, that trip "... someday may be made overnight—who knows?"

Donovan Smith,
Craig Elementary School.
Teacher Janice Lund

Believe it or not, the very first airplane to come to Alaska traveled by **boat** in 1913. It was all in pieces and had to be put together like a plywood glider.

To understand the difference in time and trouble between air and land travel, consider the first Alaska air mail flight. The mail was delivered by pilot Carl Ben Eielson (1897-1929) in February, 1924. In his DeHaviland plane, Eielson raced a mail carrier traveling by dog sled on the ground. Both were traveling from Fairbanks to McGrath, 300 miles one way.

Once in the air, Eielson saw the regular mail carrier and dog sled below him. They had just started to cross 16-mile-long Lake Minchumina heading for McGrath, too. Eielson flew against a heavy wind, delivered the mail at McGrath, took care of some business, celebrated the first flight with friends, and headed back toward Fairbanks. When he reached the lake, the dog sled team below was still crossing it!

Planes flew more slowly then. There were no seat belts, no radios, no electronic navigation. There were no landing field lights when it got dark. There were no landing fields! Landing meant finding a flat beach, or a strip of treeless land, or a frozen lake to set down on. No one knew how cold temperatures would affect the plane engines either. Flying was a risky business.

Carl Ben Eielson with an early airplane.

JIM RUOTSALA COLLECTION

People who ran hotels on the ground—roadhouses—did not like pilots in those days. The flyers took business away from their inns. The roadhouse owners sometimes posted signs outside their doors. The signs said "No Dogs or Pilots Allowed Inside."

But for Alaska, flying was the fast and glorious way to go.

No Alaskan woman had a pilot's license then. It was not until 1927 that Marvel Crosson received her wings from Carl Ben Eielson.

Through the years since those first flights, planes have transported people and supplies all over Alaska, and they still do. They bring nurses and doctors to isolated villages. They deliver groceries and mail. Coast Guard helicopters pluck people from stormy oceans. Airplanes protect Alaska and the United States from foreign powers. Perhaps the only geographic problem airplanes have not conquered is the weather.

After the gold rushes brought people to Alaska, it was a time of growth. Air travel flourished and connected villages in hours. Mining developed on the Seward Peninsula, near Nome. In all of

Marvel Crosson, Alaskan Pilot
(1900-1929)

One early day Alaskan pilot was a woman. At the age of 13, Marvel Crosson saw an airplane show in Colorado, and the event fired her dream to be a pilot. At that time, it was only 10 years after planes had started flying.

Both Marvel and her brother Joe learned to fly in California. Later they came to Alaska. Every chance she had, Marvel practiced flying over the Fairbanks area.

Aviation inspector and pilot Carl Ben Eielson gave Marvel her flight examination in 1927. He issued her a pilot's license. Marvel was the first woman in the Territory of Alaska to receive her wings. After that, she was busy delivering supplies by air from her Fairbanks headquarters.

In the summer of 1929, Marvel entered the National Women's Air Derby. On her flight over Arizona, she had some kind of plane trouble and tried to bail out. However, she was too close to the ground for her parachute to open. Officials found her wrecked plane, and her body, close by.

As the first woman flyer in Alaska, Marvel Crosson broke the trail for other women pilots to follow.

Photo ALASKA AVIATION HERITAGE MUSEUM, CROSSON COLLECTION

ALASKA STATE LIBRARY, MARY NAN GAMBLE COLLECTION

During the Great Depression in 1935, the U.S. government helped 200 families try to start new lives farming in the fertile Matanuska Valley.

Alaska there were about 60,000 people. Most lived along the coast, although Fairbanks in the interior was growing, too.

Many people down south still thought of Alaska as a far away place with snow, and people living in igloos. That's why some were surprised during the Great Depression when the U.S. government sent about 200 families to the Matanuska Valley to farm. That was in 1935. The Valley was protected by mountains near Anchorage, with mild temperatures, good soil, and enough rain for farming. During the long, warm days of light in summer, vegetables grew to giant sizes.

But it was not peaceful farming that brought many more people to Alaska. It was war.

The Japanese invasion of the Aleutian Islands brought U.S. troops to Attu in May 1943. Today, rusty reminders of the invasion can still be seen on Aleutian beaches.

13 The Military in Alaska

When the Japanese bombed Hawaii in 1941, the United States declared war. Parts of Alaska's Aleutian Islands, however, are even closer to Japan than Hawaii is.

Japan landed army forces on Attu Island in the Aleutians so it could have a foothold on the North American continent. Japanese leaders thought having a base there would help keep the Americans from invading Japan.

ALASKA STATE LIBRARY, U.S. ARMY SIGNAL CORPS COLLECTION

AMNWR, ROBERT ANGELL

At the beginning of World War II, Alaska was not ready for war. The only thing close to a military base in Alaska at that time was a barracks near Haines. Just 300 men stayed there. The distance between Haines and Attu Island was 2,700 miles. That's almost like having 300 soldiers in Miami, Florida, to protect people in Seattle, with no military help between. The distance is the same.

The United States government realized that American soldiers were needed in Alaska. Before they could come, however, there had to be a place for them to stay. Food and supplies had to be brought in, and so did military weapons.

People Displaced by War

When the Japanese attacked the Aleutian Islands, a few Native people were taken to Japan as prisoners. Hastily, the U.S. government moved more than 800 Native people from the Aleutian and Pribilof Islands to keep them safe from enemy forces. Some people were relocated to five places in southeastern Alaska. Although the U.S. government resettled these Aleut people, it did not provide well for them. The people lived out the war in hardship, only later to return to their ruined homes on the islands.

Photo, ALASKA STATE LIBRARY, BUTLER/DALE COLLECTION

The Territory needed a steady stream of supplies to defend Alaska and the rest of North America. Soon there was a scramble to build military bases, landing fields, and seaports. The U.S. government had talked for years about building a road to Alaska. Now, it **had** to be built.

Since the road would have to cross through Canada, an agreement was made with the Canadian government. In 1942-43 the 1,500-mile Alaska-Canada Military Highway (called "The Alcan") was built in nine months! It was a rough road, but it served its purpose.

The Alaska-Canada Military Highway

NATIONAL ARCHIVES, WASHINGTON, D.C.

The Alaska section of the Alcan was built by the all-Black 97th Division of the U.S. Army Corps of Engineers. The 97th pushed through a 1,500-mile pioneer road in 8 months and 12 days. Most experts had predicted the road couldn't be built at all.

Think about this. In 1972, with all our modern technology, it took more than two years to build the North Slope haul road 300 miles from Fairbanks to Prudhoe Bay. To build the Alcan, which is five times longer, in just nine months, was a miracle.

Constructing the Alcan was a battle with mud, mosquitoes, dust, permafrost, rivers, mountains, trees, and bears. It meant working 24 hours a day, seven days a week, with poor maps, trying to get done before winter arrived. Whew! Such construction had never been done before.

Author Froelich Rainey wrote in the February 1943 issue of *National Geographic* magazine:

> *If I were asked to design a monument commemorating the construction of the Alcan Highway, I would model a 20-ton caterpillar tractor driven by two soldiers, one negro and one white, but so greasy and grimy that the difference in color would be practically imperceptible. Just ahead of the machine and its drivers, I would place a tattered and bewhiskered officer riding knee to knee with a Canadian Indian, both mounted upon jaded and bony cayuses [horses].*

After World War II, many military people left Alaska. Some remained at such places as Elmendorf Air Force Base in Anchorage and Eielson Air Force Base in Fairbanks.

Because of the military, seaports, air fields, and communication systems had been improved. More people thought living in Alaska might be all right. By 1950, the population in Alaska had mushroomed to 128,000.

U.S AIR FORCE, RANDY JOLLY

Because of its geographic location, Alaska is very important to United States military security.

Even during the war, it was certain the United States and its western neighbor, the Soviet Union (USSR), were not getting along. These resentful feelings continued after the war. Each country had strongly different ideas about how governments should be run. No bombs were dropped, but people were afraid they might be. Suspicions and bad feelings developed into the Cold War, which lasted until the 1990s.

Because the United States and the USSR were located close together, the U.S. decided to strengthen military bases in Alaska. In the early 1950s a Distant Early Warning System (nicknamed the DEW line) and other defenses were built along Alaska's coast and in the interior. Once again, Alaska's geographic location made it important to United States military security. That is still so today.

In the 1990s, the U.S. and Russia became friendlier neighbors. However, both nations continue to operate highly modern security systems. More than 25,000 people continue to work in Alaska for the U.S. military.

CHARLES MASON

Before the fall of the Berlin Wall, American Cub Scouts from Nome visited the Soviet Union. Near Provideniya in the Soviet Far East they shared a hot dog roast with Soviet Young Pioneers.

14 Statehood, Land Claims, and The Oil Boom

Alaska became the 49th State in January 1959. From that time on, Alaskans could pass laws and do many things without asking the U.S. Congress.

Up to the time of statehood, the federal government in Washington, D.C., managed the

Courtesy ED AND NANCY FERRELL

101

land in Alaska. Congress made decisions on how Alaskan lands and waters were used. When Alaska became a state, Alaskan leaders were allowed to choose millions of acres of land to manage. Controlling these lands and making rules about them would help Alaskans build their own state.

Alaskan lawmakers had to be careful when making decisions. They wanted to make money for the state by using its natural resources. At the same time, they wanted to save resources so they would not be used up. There had to be a balance.

In any case, Alaskans were soon hired for government jobs, and state departments grew. People got busy working and managing their own state.

ALASKA STATE LIBRARY, EARLY PRINTS COLLECTION, R. N. DeARMOND

Not all Alaskans were in favor of statehood, but many celebrated the event. They believed being part of the United States would make their lives better.

Businessmen then looked to develop other Alaska resources. In 1958 oil and gas fields had been discovered on the Kenai Peninsula. Then in 1968, private companies found oil underground at Prudhoe Bay in the Arctic.

The oil companies wanted to drill for oil in Alaska. But nobody really knew who owned the arctic land. Before companies could drill, they had to be sure they could own or borrow the land.

During the years of Russian control, and even after the United States bought Alaska, the Native people had had little say about how Alaska grew. Their ancient relatives had been in Alaska first, and Natives felt they had a claim on Alaska's land.

Through the years, Alaska's Indians, Eskimos, and Aleuts had tried to be heard. However, many were not familiar with the new ways of government. Most of them lived far from the new towns and cities. Native people and newcomers did not understand each other or the way they each lived. Sometimes there were bad feelings among different groups, too.

At last in 1966 all the Native groups joined together in the Alaska Federation of Natives. They insisted that they owned the land the oil companies wanted to use. It was important to their traditional ways of life. Before Natives would share use of the land, they wanted payment in some form.

In 1971 the U.S. Congress passed the Alaska Native Claims Settlement Act (ANCSA). Native people and their village governments chose 44 million acres of land they wanted to own, and they could do what they wanted with it. They

PETER METCALFE

Native village and regional corporations created by the Alaska Native Claims Settlement Act (1971) are governed by their shareholders. These people are considering important decisions at a meeting of the Kootznoowoo Native (village) corporation in Angoon.

Alaska Native Regional Corporations

The twelve Alaska Native regional corporations are:
    Ahtna Incorporated
    Aleut Corporation
    Arctic Slope Regional Corporation
    Bering Straits Native Corporation
    Bristol Bay Native Corporation
    Calista Corporation
    Chugach Natives, Inc.
    Cook Inlet Region, Inc.
    Doyon Limited
    Koniag, Inc.
    NANA Regional Corporation, Inc.
    Sealaska Corporation
A thirteenth corporation for Natives living outside Alaska is in Seattle, Washington.

DOUGLAS YATES

The TransAlaska Pipeline was built to carry oil 800 miles from Prudhoe Bay, near the Beaufort Sea, to Valdez on Prince William Sound.

received nearly a billion dollars to help make up for the land they gave up. They formed 12 regional *corporations* to create Native businesses and other projects to help the people. Once the Native land claims were settled, oil companies prepared to drill for oil.

Getting the oil to markets outside Alaska was a big problem. Taking the oil by ship around Alaska seemed impossible. Remember, the coastline is longer than the whole U.S. coastline. Besides, some northern waters freeze or have floating ice most of the year.

Companies decided to build a pipeline—directly across Alaska—to carry the oil. The pipeline would extend from the oil fields at Prudhoe Bay in northern Alaska to Valdez, with its port on Prince William Sound. From there it would be carried south in huge ships called supertankers.

Some people did not want this pipeline. They were afraid it would damage the land and the animals. They said it might accidentally spill oil. But lawmakers decided it was all right, as long as certain rules were followed to protect the environment.

The oil companies hired people from all over the United States to build the oil field and the pipeline. They offered high wages for working

LOWER KUSKOKWIM SCHOOL DISTRICT

The Anna Tobeluk School in Nunapitchuk is named after a young girl who did not want to leave her home to go to high school. In the mid-1970s, Anna and some other young people sued the State of Alaska because there were no high school programs in their small communities. In response, the State used profits from the oil boom to build more than 120 new schools in rural Alaska.

long hours in the extreme cold and the wilderness. Thousands of people hurried to Alaska to take the high paying jobs. Houses were built for them to live in. Stores were built to feed and clothe them. Construction was going on everywhere.

All this activity created a *boom*, a time of frantic activity and large profits for some people. It was like the Russian rush for furs and the gold rush stampedes. Alaska's population increased by about 30,000 people. Most of the growth was in the southcentral part of the state, especially Valdez and Anchorage. Some was in Fairbanks.

The Prudhoe Bay oil actually belonged to the state of Alaska, so the oil companies had to pay taxes to the state. Suddenly, Alaska could afford to build more schools, highways, and air fields. Money from the oil supported the state for years, and it still does today.

It is interesting to know about the very first supertanker cargo of "black gold." It was sent to the U.S. West Coast from Valdez in 1977. The oil in the tanker was worth $7.2 million. That alone—that one tanker load of oil—was the price of Alaska when the Russians sold it in 1867.

"Supertankers" such as this one carry oil from Alaska to markets in the continental U.S.

ALASKA DIVISION OF TOURISM

ROLLO POOL

Some Alaska Native Corporations harvest logs from their land to export from Alaska. These men are loading logs in Ketchikan for the Cape Fox Native Corporation.

15   The Importance of Timber

Because of Alaska's varied geography, trees do not grow all over the state. But where they do grow, people have been using them for centuries. Natives used them for houses. Russians used them to build ships. Stampeders built log cabins. Even today, an important number of Alaskans build with wood or use it for fuel.

Companies have been logging, or cutting trees to send outside Alaska, since World War I. Most of the logging has taken place in the lush coastal forests of southeastern Alaska. To promote jobs through the years, the U.S. government arranged for two pulp mills to be built in the 1950s. One was in Ketchikan, one in Sitka.

Many of the logged spruce and hemlock trees along the southeastern coast were 400 to 600 years old. That means some of the trees started growing long before explorers landed in Alaska. About half of the trees cut down were ground into pulp to make paper and rayon. The rest were cut into logs. The pulp and most of the logs were shipped out of state, largely to Japan.

However, the Southeast is not the only place in Alaska where there are forests. There are many trees in the interior and along the coast of southcentral Alaska. Government and private landowners are developing these forests, too.

A number of people today think too many of Alaska's trees are being cut too fast. They say the new forests that grow in place of the old ones are not the same for hundreds of years. The new growing forests do not make a healthy environment for animals, fish, and plants. They think pulp mills pollute the air and water too much.

Other people say trees must be cut to make jobs and money for families. It is a hard problem to solve, as there is something to say for each side.

Commercial Forests

Source: Alaska Dept. of Commerce and Economic Development

Alaska has large areas of forests, but only a portion of them are of commercial value.

16 Tourism

Ever since the 1880s, people have sailed to Alaska to see the variety of landscapes, animals, and ways of life. Traveling was expensive in those days, and it took a long time. Not many people could afford it.

In this day of air travel, it takes just a few hours to reach Alaska from Seattle. Traveling is easier. More people can afford vacations. After their trips, tourists go home and tell other people about their adventures. Then more people want to come.

Tourists may not live in Alaska, but they help support people who do. While tourists are in Alaska, they need services such as places to stay, food, transportation, clothing, and gifts. (If your relatives go

Tourism provides jobs for Alaskans.

ALASKA DIVISION OF TOURISM, MARK WAYNE

ALASKA DIVISION OF TOURISM

A great number of tourists buy "package" tours and come to Alaska by cruise ships. A tour package may include train, bus, and small plane trips to sightseeing spots. Because of this, many of the sights visitors see are the ones easy to reach near waterways in southeastern and southcentral Alaska.

Alaska's Top Ten Attractions

1. The Inside Passage, Ketchikan to Skagway
2. Mendenhall Glacier, Juneau
3. Glacier Bay National Park
4. Historic Skagway
5. Totem Parks in Ketchikan
6. Portage Glacier, near Anchorage
7. Denali National Park
8. Anchorage Museum of History and Art
9. University of Alaska Fairbanks
10. The TransAlaska Pipeline

someplace, don't they often bring you back a present?) They need people to help plan their trips. Taking care of tourists makes jobs for Alaskans in what is called the service industry.

Whether they come by jet, small plane, ferry, cruise ship, motorcycle, motorhome, or car, tourists spark growth in businesses and transportation. Most of the visitors come in the summertime. Some tourists even come back and stay.

What do tourists like to see most? Geography, of course. The Inside Passage of southeastern Alaska is most popular. Next are glaciers and totem poles. Viewing Mt. McKinley is high on the list, too.

Though many tourists like to look at Alaska's highlights, others enjoy the "doing" aspect of geography. Tourists travel from all points of the world to, say, hunt the Kodiak country, or fish in Kenai streams, or kayak the Noatak River to Kotzebue Sound. People have built lodges and hunting camps especially for those kinds of tourists. In total numbers, twice as many tourists come to Alaska every year as there are people living in the state.

Where do most visitors come from? From California, Washington, Texas, and Florida, in that order. A great number come from other countries, as well.

However, don't forget: Alaskans are tourists also. If you take a train to Denali Park, or fly to Nome to see the end of the Iditarod Sled Dog

Race, or drive to Anchorage to look over the aviation museum, you are a kind of tourist, too. School classes from all over the state sometimes travel to experience the sights and activities of different places.

17 Providing Services for Alaskans

It takes many people to keep the State of Alaska and its towns and villages running smoothly.

More Alaskans are busy in local, state, and federal work than in any other jobs. Perhaps your mother or father works for the state or teaches in a school. If you include military people, about 96,000 Alaskans are now employed in government jobs of some kind.

Look in the front of your telephone book sometime, if you have one where you live. It will tell you some of the benefits government provides—such as police and fire protection, health services, schools, and so much more.

In addition, all Alaskan workers and their families have everyday needs where they live. Because they buy food, get their hair cut, purchase clothing, rent videos, bank money, use laundromats, need dentists, plus more, jobs are created for other Alaskans.

The people who fill these needs work in the service industry. They provide services for themselves and for other people. Look

DOUGLAS YATES

People in rural areas sometimes find jobs showing tourists how they live in "the bush."

People who work for airports, airlines, hospitals, and city government do important work for their communities.

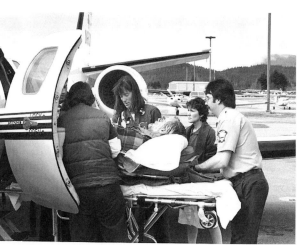
PETER METCALFE

DOUGLAS YATES

Some Alaskans make a living by providing their neighbors with food and other supplies.

around when you go to town, and you'll see this for yourself. You will see restaurants, banks, grocery stores, and other businesses.

As people in all jobs traveled north to live, the population of Alaska continued to grow. In 1994, it reached the 600,000 mark.

You see that for thousands of years people have been coming to Alaska. They came across the land bridge, then by sea from Asia, from Europe, and from the Americas.

People came because of what was in the seas, on the land, and beneath the ground. They came because of Alaska's **geography!** In the next chapters, we will look closely at how people's lives are still being influenced by Alaska's geography. Follow closely as we zero in on the various regions of the state.

Suggested Reading

Bayson, Jamie. *The War Canoe.* Anchorage: Alaska Northwest Books, 1990.

A young Tlingit Indian discovers his proud heritage and builds a war canoe to honor the discovery of this heritage.

Beattie, Owen. *Buried in Ice.* N.Y.: Scholastic/Madison Press Books, 1992.

Probes the tragic and mysterious fate of Sir John Franklin's failed expedition to find the Northwest Passage in 1845.

DeArmond, Dale. *Berry Woman's Children.* N.Y.: Greenwillow Books, 1985.

Brief retellings of Eskimo animal legends.

Jenness, Aylette. *In Two Worlds.* Boston: Houghton Mifflin Co., 1989.

Life of a Yupik Eskimo family on the Bering Sea, detailing the changes that have taken place in the last 50 years.

Jessell, Tim. *Amorak.* Mankato, Mn.: Creative Editions, 1994.

An Inuit grandfather explains, through an old story, how the caribou and the wolf are brothers even though one hunts the other.

Lourie, Peter. *Yukon River.* Honesdale, Pa.: Caroline House, 1992.

The author takes a trip down the Yukon River by canoe, following the old gold rush route.

Murphy, Claire Rudolf. *A Child's Alaska.* Seattle: Alaska Northwest Books, 1994.

A written and pictorial overview of Alaska's animals, land forms, cultures, and activities.

Murphy, Claire Rudolf. *The Prince and the Salmon People.* N.Y.: Rizzoli, 1993.

When salmon stop coming to his village, a Tsimshian prince travels to the world of the Spring Salmon people and discovers the vital connection between the human and animal worlds. Includes lifestyle information.

Paulsen, Gary. *Dogsong.* N.Y.: Bradbury Press, 1985.

An Eskimo teenager takes his dog team on a jorney of self-discovery, where he uses his survival skills to save another.

Rogers, Jean. *Goodbye My Island.* N.Y.: Greenwillow Books, 1983.

Twelve-year-old Esther Atoolik tells of the last winter her people spent on King Island, Alaska, in the early 1960s.

Ungerman, Kenneth. *The Race To Nome.* N.Y.: Harper and Row, 1993, 1963.

Tells of the diphtheria epidemic in Nome, and those who saved the people there.

Shemie, Bonnie. *Houses of Snow, Skin and Bones.* Montreal, Canada: Tundra Books, 1989.

A basic description of tools, area, and houses of the Arctic.

Sis, Peter. *A Small Tall Tale from the Far Far North.* N.Y.: Knopf. Distributed by Random House, 1993.

With the help of Eskimos, Jan Wetzl survives a perilous journey from Central Europe to the arctic regions in the late 1800s.

Jill Campbell and Denise Haviland, Gambell Elementary School. Teachers Mechelle Andrews and Peter Sutch.

PART 3

Five Regions
of Alaska Today

Why Regions Are Important

W hen states or countries are very large, or when parts of them are quite different, it is helpful to separate them into areas called **regions.**

To help understand this idea, think about your school. Inside, areas are organized into rooms by grades. Or rooms are organized by activity, such as music or library work. Each room could be called a "region" of the building. The school was especially divided like that for a reason.

In the world outside your school, nature is often the divider. Many times geographic features such as mountains or rivers become natural dividers. For instance, the Cascade Mountains in the Lower 48 States separate Oregon's rainy coast from its eastern deserts. The Rio Grande River separates Texas from Mexico.

Parts of Alaska can be separated the same way, by regions. There are such differences in climate, land forms, animals, and people you cannot talk about one region as if it were like all the others. Yet many things within a single region can be very much alike, too.

NANCY RABENER

Mountains separate most of Alaska's regions. This is the Alaska Range seen from near Delta in Interior Alaska.

- Far North
- Western
- Interior
- Southcentral
- Southeast

Five Regions of Alaska

Gillnetting for herring in Bristol Bay   JIM NILSEN

113

Often mountains make good dividers between regions, as in Alaska. The high peaks affect the climate of a region and the animals and plants that grow there. The mountains help decide how and why people live where they do.

Some people separate Alaska into five regions. When you imagine that Alaska is shaped like the side view of a mammoth's head, the regions have a pattern. The top of the mammoth's head would be the **Far North** Region. The mammoth's face and tusks would be the **Western** region. The side of the mammoth's head, where the ear is, would be the **Interior** region.

The mammoth's chin would be the **Southcentral** region. The neck would be the **Southeast** region.

Mountains are the main geographic feature that set apart Alaska's regions. The Brooks Range separates the Far North from the Interior; the Alaska Range separates the Interior from Southcentral; and the Coast Range separates Southeast from Canada.

Note. You will notice one other thing about regions as you read through the following chapters: Once a name is given to a region, that name is capitalized as a proper noun or adjective because it refers to a specific place.

Michelle Tungiyan, Davinda Ohktokiyuk, Dawny James, Gambell Elementary School. Teachers Mechelle Andrews and Peter Sutch

The Far North Region

If your school were in Barrow or Kaktovik, you might see a polar bear pass by in the distance. In fact, some bears come into town looking for food. Not many students in the world get to see a real polar bear that close.

In the winter, you would wear a heavy parka outside. Temperatures stay well below zero. When the winds blow, which happens often, it feels even colder. In summer you need a jacket, too, but then temperatures are usually closer to 40°F and 50°F above zero.

Still, most of the time it is cold in this arctic region. Since the earth tips away from the sun in the winter, much of the Arctic is dark for at least two months. In the brief summertime, daylight may last for nearly three months. That means 24 hours of daylight every day.

Harold Kaveolook

Years ago the U.S. Bureau of Indian Affairs asked Harold Kaveolook to start a school in Kaktovik. He and the Inupiaq villagers collected wood and built one. Harold was its teacher for many years. Now there is a brand new elementary school in Kaktovik, and it is named in honor of him.

Harold Kaveolook
School, Kaktovik

NORTH SLOPE BOROUGH SCHOOL DISTRICT

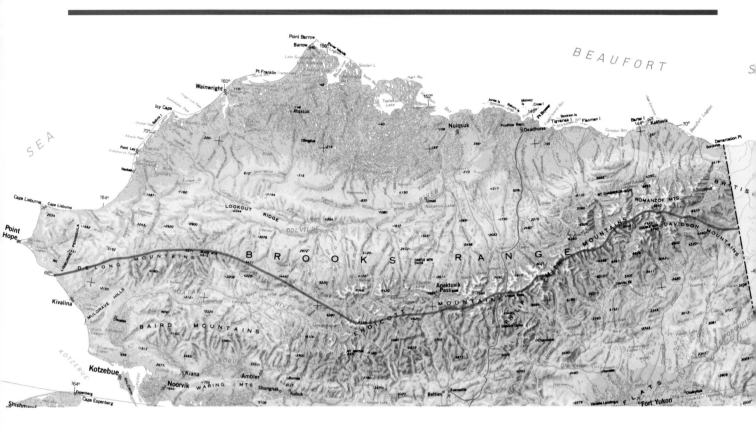

The flat arctic coastal plain is often cold and windy.

NANCY RABENER

1   Where Is It?

The Far North Region is really a broad strip of land crowning Alaska. It is the top of the Alaska mammoth's head you are picturing in your mind. In the south the mountains of the Brooks Range divide this region from the rest of the state.

2   What Is There?

The high peaks of the Brooks Range sweep east to west from Canada to the Chukchi Sea, clear across Alaska. On the north side the mountains slope down to hills, and then to flat tundra along the arctic coast. This area, often called the "North Slope," extends some 200 miles north to the Arctic

Ocean. Many of the region's people live along its shore. This is a cold land. In summer the sea ice melts back from the coast, but the ice never disappears entirely.

The area's largest river is the Colville. This river winds across the land carrying rain and melted snow to the Beaufort Sea. Rivers are especially important in this region. They are important not only for travel and fishing, but as landmarks. In an area as flat as the Far North, a landmark of any kind helps to tell a traveler which direction to go.

DOUGLAS YATES

The Sagavanirktok River winds across the northern tundra. It flows into the Beaufort Sea near Prudhoe Bay.

3   The Northern Tundra

There are no trees in the Far North. This is tundra area, with permafrost under the top soil. The few inches of rain that fall during the year stay on top of the ground. If a river floods, the water cannot sink into the frozen ground. The spreading water makes the soil spongy, or it lies on top and forms puddles or lakes. In summer, mosquitoes love that moisture. They are great pests to humans and animals, but they make tasty meals for tundra birds.

ALASKA DIVISION OF TOURISM, ERNEST SCHNEIDER

People have learned that putting big, soft tires on vehicles helps keep them from damaging the delicate tundra.

Grasses, lichens and mosses grow in lowlands on the tundra. Tiny, colorful plants burst out in the summer. Their lives are short, but they produce flowers, roots, and berries. Willow trees and low bushes are often found along streams. Brush and bushes grow on hills at the foot of the mountains.

The tundra is fragile. Removing or disturbing its plants or soil causes the permafrost underneath to melt. During the summer, tires on vehicles driving over the soil can damage the plant growth. The land may not recover for years. Only tires with very low pressure do not hurt the fragile plants. In winter when there are snow and ice, tires are not harmful because the earth is hard.

Grizzly bears on the tundra are smaller than their cousins that live along the coast. They have to roam far in search of food. They may spend six or seven months a year asleep in their dens.

DOUGLAS YATES

4 The Animals There

Did you think there would be few animals in the Far North? Not at all! Animals such as caribou, bears, wolves, arctic hares, lemmings, and wolverines feel that area is just right for them. Loons, geese, ducks, and swans mate, nest, and raise their young during the summer. They migrate south for the winter. In the ocean or along the ice, there are polar bears, whales, seals, and walruses.

What do animals eat in this seemingly sparse land? Some eat the tiny plants on the tundra. Some eat insects. Some eat shellfish in the nearby sea. And some eat **each other** to survive.

Herds of caribou migrate to the tundra every spring through passes in the Brooks Range. Here the U.S. government has put aside land called the Arctic National Wildlife Refuge. Saving these lands will help make sure animals such as the caribou have a place to live in the future.

5 The People There

In spite of the harsh climate, people have lived in the Far North for thousands of years. Scientists have found ancient tools at Walakpa Bay, 10 miles south of Barrow. These relics date back to 2,500 B.C.! Remains from other early people have been found along the coast, too. The Inupiaq people who live in the Arctic today have ancient family ties. They come from families who have lived in the area for more than 1,000 years.

Howard Rock
Native Leader
(1911-1976)

Inupiaq Howard Rock was born at Point Hope in 1911. In those days, young students had to dip pens into ink to have them write. It was so cold in Howard's school, the ink froze in the bottle.

Howard was the only one in his family who learned to read. He would read fairy tales and then tell them to his family. From the beginning, he loved words and books. Education was important to him. When he was older, he started the Native newspaper, the *Tundra Times*. As editor of the *Times*, he fought for the rights of Native Alaskans.

Howard Rock was not only good with words. He was also an outstanding artist, as you can see in his oil painting, "The Dance of Kakairnok."

ANCHORAGE MUSEUM OF HISTORY AND ART

North Slope students learn subjects and skills from many nations and cultures.

NORTH SLOPE BOROUGH SCHOOL DISTRICT

Students also learn traditional subsistence skills.

NORTH SLOPE BOROUGH SCHOOL DISTRICT

About 7,400 people reside in the Far North. That is a small portion of Alaska's total population. Most people live in settlements along the coast. A few people live in villages inland.

Barrow is the largest town in the region. Its population has grown during the last 20 years with the oil pipeline activity at Prudhoe Bay. About 4,000 people live in Barrow now. Most of the people are Native Inupiaqs. Others come from families of European, Mexican, Jamaican, Filipino, Korean, or African American heritage. Barrow is very modern, and people come there from all parts of the world.

Even today most Inupiaq people in the Far North choose to live at least partly by subsistence. That means they survive by hunting, fishing, and gathering from the land and sea around them. They believe that way of life not only keeps the body alive, but also fills important needs of the inner spirit.

People in inland villages live mostly by hunting caribou and fishing in the rivers. One village, Anaktuvuk Pass, grew where it did because that is where caribou pass on their migration through the Brooks Range.

People in coastal villages such as Point Hope live by hunting whales and other sea mammals. The village has been located for many generations on the point of land where whales pass each year during their migrations.

Whaling captains from Point Hope and other Native villages serve on the Alaska Eskimo Whaling Commission. That international group helps decide how many whales it is safe to take for subsistence.

It is interesting how Natives handle this balance. Before the season, it is decided how many whales it would be safe to take. Each whale is called a "strike." Depending on how many people live there, villages along the whale migration route are given permission for so many "strikes," or attempts to kill a whale. If a village does not use all its strikes as the whales swim by, it can pass them on to another village along the migration route. In this way, people somewhere can make use of the total number of whales allowed, but everyone is staying within the limits set beforehand. This protects the populations of whales for the future.

ALASKA DIVISION OF TOURISM

Harvesting whales is an important part of life for people in the Far North.

You might wonder, since the arctic coast is so flat, how the people in early whaling villages knew when whales were coming through. One way may have started a tradition.

If you have heard of the "blanket toss," you may have the answer. In this activity, a circle of people holds a blanket made of bearded seal skins parallel to the ground. Then they bounce a person

Many artists have been fascinated with the blanket toss. This print is by Juneau artist Rie Muñoz and is called "The Creation of Man."

on it high into the air. Some people believe the blanket toss started as a way for someone to spot whales far in the distance. Now it is part of a community celebration after the whaling season is over.

Besides living by subsistence, people in the Far North may earn a living working at government jobs, in schools, in stores, on construction projects, or for the village and regional Native corporations. Still, many people prefer to live a subsistence lifestyle at least part of the time.

6 Oil in the Arctic

Inupiaq people have known there was oil in the region for hundreds of years. They used it themselves for fires to heat their homes. The U.S. government learned of arctic oil during the 1900s. Underground gas was found, too. In 1923 the federal government put aside 37,000 square miles of land as an oil reserve that might later be used for drilling.

Nobody paid much attention to oil in the Far North until World War II. Then gas and oil were used by both the U.S. Navy and by Inupiaqs. In 1968 oil companies found rich oil fields on state land at Prudhoe Bay. This area is along the coast of the Beaufort Sea. It was, experts said, the largest oil field ever found in North America.

Building a pipeline to carry the oil to the port of Valdez was a gigantic project. It was like building a pipeline from Chicago to New York City, a distance of 800 miles. A road, now called the Dalton Highway, had to be built to bring supplies and workers north from the Yukon River. All that had to be done across wilderness and mountains, across streams and rivers, and in some of the coldest weather on earth.

ALASKA DIVISION OF TOURISM

The TransAlaska Pipeline extends 800 miles from the Far North to Southcentral Alaska.

What about permafrost? Alaskans asked. What about the delicate tundra and the animals ranging the area? What if the pipeline broke and oil spilled all over the land?

An oil drilling rig at Prudhoe Bay.

JOHN TUCKEY

NANCY RABENER

The TransAlaska Pipeline is heavily insulated where it passes through permafrost.

A lot of questions had to be answered.

People were especially concerned about disturbing the land and the animals. Inupiaq and Athabaskan people were worried because they depend on both for their subsistence way of life.

When the pipeline was finally built, part of it was insulated. Also, about half of it was built several feet above ground. That kept the permafrost from being disturbed. In places, the pipe was high enough that animals such as caribou on their migrations could travel underneath. The work was completed in 1977.

7 Old Ways and New

Because of oil company construction, many changes have come to Barrow and the North Slope. Modern schools, television, satellite communications, and other technologies were brought in.

New technologies have even tamed the permafrost a bit. Strong building equipment can now bite into the rock-like soil and dig down. New types of insulation help protect the fragile permafrost. Because of this, a "Utilidor" pipe system was constructed in some parts of Barrow. Insulated water pipes and sewer pipes were laid below ground, even though years ago that would have seemed impossible.

NORTH SLOPE BOROUGH

Barrow's Utilidor system carried underground water and sewer pipes through permafrost. It has been replaced by an even more advanced system.

On the other hand, permafrost prevents disposal of trash. Trash cannot be treated and buried as in warmer areas of the state. Thus, pollution is a problem. Far North people are concerned, and are always working on ways to solve this problem.

Whether living in towns or villages, many Inupiaqs are happy with traditional ways of living. They do not want their subsistence lifestyle disturbed.

Nowadays, people follow both old ways and new ways in Barrow. People may hunt for seals, whales, or caribou, but they use computers and travel around on snowmachines, too. A few third grade students at Ipalook Elementary School told of the combined lifestyles in a recent report:

NORTH SLOPE BOROUGH

Today borough employees in the Far North use computerized Geographic Information Systems to study how the land should be used.

Barrow is the biggest village. Barrow is at the top of the world.

It is fun in the summer. You can go swimming at the Barrow High School. It has a deep end and a shallow end. You can go to the stores with your friends…You have good food to eat, such as vegetables.

There are a lot of whales at the beach in the water. They are very big. There are fourteen whales to hunt this year. The whales are dark black and white. I like the polar bears, because they are white and big. There are a lot of foxes and snow owls around Barrow. There are also seals, fish, walruses, and caribou near Barrow.

Joey Dingman, Greta Stuermer, Bobbi Brower, and Elli Ebue,
Ipalook Elementary, Barrow. Teacher Steven Bigler

NORTH SLOPE BOROUGH SCHOOL DISTRICT

People in the Far North follow both old ways and new.

Now, from the Far North Region, fly west to the face of the Alaska mammoth. There you will find the Western Region facing the Pacific Ocean.

Suggested Reading

Andrews, Jan. *The Very Last First Time.* N.Y.: A Margaret McElderry Book, 1986.

> A young Inuit (Canadian) girl gathers sea food under the sea ice when the tide is out.

Kalman, Bobbie and Ken Ferris. *Arctic Whales and Whaling.* N.Y.: Crabtree Publishing Co., 1988.

> A description of whales and whaling, whale uses, how they have been hunted, plus environmental issues.

Matthews, Downs. *Arctic Summer.* N.Y.: Simon & Schuster Books for Young Readers, 1993.

> Tells of an unusual landscape bursting with life and color—animals, tundra, sea life, camouflage.

Pandell, Karen. *Land of Dark, Land of Light.* N.Y.: Dutton Children's Books, 1993.

> Animals and plants of the Arctic throughout the year, with focus on the Arctic National Wildlife Refuge (no map).

The Western Region

If you lived in the Western Region, you might need several different kinds of jackets. The weather varies from very cold to mild and wet. That means parkas to warm boots to rain gear.

But no matter what the weather, school is never called off here. Especially not in Toksook Bay on the Bering Sea.

Except once.

It might be 10°F below zero. Snow could be blowing. The wind off the ocean could be roaring at 70 miles an hour. Kids going to school might have to hold onto clotheslines to stay together and find their way. But school would still be open. If the weather gets really bad, parents might run their kids to school on snowmachines, but school is never called off.

Except on one wild, snowy day when wind and snow made practically a whiteout. That time there was no school—because the **principal** couldn't find the building!

Auntie Mary Nicoli
The elementary school at Aniak is named after hard-working Auntie Mary Nicoli. She was called "Auntie" because she was always looking after kids and was "Auntie" to other members of the community as well.

Auntie Mary Nicoli Elementary School, Aniak

KUSPUK SCHOOLS

NANCY RABENER

Weather in the Western Region can be bitterly cold and windy.

Parts of the Western Region are rich in minerals. The Red Dog Mine near Kotzebue is the largest producer of zinc in the world.

STEVE KESSLER

1   Where Is It?

Toksook Bay is only one community in the Western Region. This region is the face and tusks on the Alaska mammoth in your mind picture.

The region starts at the western edge of the Far North, at Kotzebue Sound on the Chukchi Sea. It includes all of Alaska that touches the Bering Sea. It also includes Kodiak Island in the south, the long Aleutian Island Chain, and the smaller islands north of those. It is bordered on the east by Interior Alaska and by a small portion of the Southcentral Region.

In many geographic ways, the Western Region has just about everything. It has islands, seacoast, rivers, mountains, peninsulas, lagoons, and even sand dunes. Its people are from Yupik, Inupiaq, Aleut, Athabaskan, and many non-Native cultures.

No roads connect villages of the Western Region with other Alaska regions. Boats and planes are the main methods of transportation. Small "bush" planes do practically everything. They land on wheels, floats, or skis, depending on the season. They fly people out and back for medical help, for vacations, for school trips, or to visit relatives. Until recent times, each village was fairly isolated. Today radios, telephones, computers, and satellite television bring instant contact with almost anyplace in the world.

Kotzebue is a major trading center for the Western Region.

STEVE KESSLER

2   A Tour By Bush Plane

To get a feeling for this varied and exciting part of Alaska, let's take a little finger tour by "bush airplane" through the region.

First, get a map. Then put your finger on Kotzebue in the north, east of the Chukchi Sea. This town of 3,000 people is headquarters for the NANA Regional Corporation. The Red Dog Mine nearby is the largest producer of zinc in the world.

The weather here is harsh. With wind and cold, the *chill factor* can reach minus 100°F! When skin is exposed to such wind, it can freeze instantly. Winter days are dark, and summer days are long and light. The land is mostly tundra, backed by rolling hills.

KOTZEBUE SOUND   Kotzebue

ST. LAWRENCE ISLAND   SEWARD PENINSULA   Nome

NORTON SOUND   Unalakleet

YUKON RIVER

Bethel   KUSKOKWIM RIVER

KUSKOKWIM BAY

Dillingham

Naknek

BRISTOL BAY   Egegik   Kodiak

ALASKA PENINSULA

KODIAK ISLAND

BERING SEA

ALEUTIAN ISLANDS   Unalaska

3 The Seward Peninsula

After a short visit, fly your finger west over the Bering Land Bridge National Preserve on the Seward Peninsula. This land is set aside to honor the coming of the ancient people and animals from Asia thousands of years ago. Not only have you flown over Kotzebue Sound to reach this Preserve, but you have crossed the Arctic Circle.

The Seward Peninsula is a great piece of land that juts far into the Bering and Chukchi Seas. The ocean here freezes in winter. It blows up such fierce storms a sea wall had to be built to keep water from flooding the city of Nome.

On land, rivers drain from the southern mountains. Many rivers

The Council City and Solomon River Railroad was built near Nome during Gold Rush days.

NANCY RABENER

contain salmon, grayling, whitefish, and arctic char. The wet lowlands rise to coastal uplands and rolling hills. There is tundra and there are lots of lakes here. It's cold in winter, but it can get warm in summer.

Before reaching Nome, on the peninsula's south side, why not drop down and relax in the Serpentine Hot Springs? They are one of nearly a hundred thermal springs throughout Alaska. The area's Inupiaq people have long enjoyed their

Reindeer Herding in Alaska

Some people think reindeer and Alaska go together. Reindeer do live in Alaska, but they were not always here.

Dr. Sheldon Jackson (1834-1909) was an American churchman and educator. He raised money and started some schools in villages of Alaska. When he was traveling the Territory in the early 1890s, he heard that Eskimos along the Bering Sea coast were starving. Jackson knew tamed reindeer of Siberia lived well in cold lands. They could be herded and kept near home, unlike the wild caribou. From then on, Jackson worked to raise money to have reindeer brought to Alaska. By 1905, the Alaska reindeer herd was doing well on the Seward Peninsula.

Mary Antisarlook, "Sinrock Mary"

An outstanding reindeer owner of those times was Mary Antisarlook (1860?-1948). She was called "Sinrock Mary." Though others tried to take her reindeer from her after her husband died, she fought to keep them. She became the first Eskimo woman to be successful in both the Native and non-Native cultures. She was rich in money by non-Native standards, but she kept the qualities important to her Eskimo culture at the same time.

Today, raising healthy reindeer provides food and jobs for a number of people in northwest Alaska. One successful herd is managed by the NANA Native corporation. For the most part, the reindeer meat is eaten locally. The antlers are shipped to Asia for use as medicine.

Photo UNIVERSITY OF ALASKA FAIRBANKS, ALASKA & POLAR REGIONS DEPT., BARRETT WILLOUGHBY COLLECTION

healthful qualities. Bush airplane pilots, too, often stopped for a quick bath on their flying trips.

You could drive the Nome-Taylor Highway south from here, but since you have a plane, it will be faster to fly.

Nome, the largest town on the Seward Peninsula, was built when miners rushed to the beaches in 1900 looking for gold nuggets. Like Kotzebue, it is a trade and transportation center for nearby villages, and a place much visited by tourists. People of many cultures mix in this northern city.

Like other buildings in permafrost areas, schools have a problem here, too. They cannot be built right on the ground. The Nome Elementary School, for example, is built on insulated pilings above the permafrost.

NANCY RABENER

In winter, people around Nome fish through the ice for tom cod.

4 St. Lawrence Island

From Nome your bush plane flies to St. Lawrence Island where Siberian Yupik people live. The International Dateline takes a jog here so the people of the island can have the same time as the rest of Alaska. It's almost the place where you can put one foot in today and the other foot in tomorrow.

If you lived on St. Lawrence, you would go to fish camp in the summer, pick salmonberries, travel by boat and snowmachine and airplane, and dance at traditional Eskimo celebrations. You would go to school, but you would go hunting, too. Here is what Gambell students tell of walrus hunting:

My village is special to me because we are famous for hunting walrus. We like walrus because they taste super good. We hunt for them at winter or spring or anytime. We use boats for walrus hunting. They're really fat and blubberish. Walruses don't feel cold because of their blubber. They have tusks like elephants. They use their tusks for fighting, climbing up on ice, and finding clams and other stuff. They're brown.

Eric Apatiki, Ben Apassingok, Roger Slwooko, Travis Kaningok, Gambell Elementary School. Teachers Mechelle Andrews and Peter Sutch

Eric Apatiki, Ben Apassingok, Roger Slwooko, Travis Kaningok

5   Along the Bering Sea Coast

Back in your plane, with your finger on the map, pilot yourself eastward, across Norton Sound, to Unalakleet. The people here live by commercial fishing and subsistence hunting and fishing.

Unalakleet is one of the stops on the great Iditarod Trail Sled Dog Race. During the race, school is called off when the first dog team arrives racing for Nome. Everyone runs to the check-in point to see who the leader is.

Now fly across the Nulato Hills and flatlands toward Bethel. You have crossed the great lowland area where the Yukon and Kuskokwim Rivers flow into the sea. Most of the people here are Yupiks. Along the rivers and on the coast, they live in small villages. Subsistence hunting, fishing, and gathering are important. So are other Yupik traditions.

Bethel, on the Kuskokwim River, is an important transportation and service center for surrounding villages.

STEVE KESSLER

NORTON SOUND

BRISTOL BAY

KUSKOKWIM BAY

ANCHORAGE

KENAI
Soldotna
Sterling
Nikiski
Homer
Seldovia
Kachemak

KODIAK
KODIAK ISLAND
Afognak Island
Port Lions
Larsen Bay

ALASKA RANGE

McGrath

Bethel
Napakiak
Napaskiak
Kwethluk
Akiak
Tuluksak
Aniak
Chuathbaluk

Hooper Bay
Chevak
Newtok
Kasigluk
Nunapitchuk
Nightmute
Chefornak
Eek
Quinhagak
Kongiganak
Kwigillingok

Emmonak
Alakanuk
Kotlik
Mountain Village
Saint Mary's
Pilot Station
Marshall
Russian Mission
Holy Cross
Grayling
Anvik
Shageluk

Stebbins
Saint Michael
Unalakleet

Tununak
Toksook Bay
Mekoryuk
Nunivak Island

Goodnews Bay
Platinum
Togiak
Manokotak
Aleknagik
Dillingham
Clarks Point
New Stuyahok
Ekwok
Naknek
King Salmon

Nondalton
Newhalen
Iliamna

ALASKA PENINSULA
ALEUTIAN RANGE

Pilot Point
Port Heiden

Chignik
Sand Point
King Cove
Cold Bay
False Pass
Unimak Island
Akutan

SHUMAGIN ISLANDS
SANAK ISLANDS
KRENITZIN ISLANDS

KILBUCK MOUNTAINS
AHKLUN MTS

WALRUS ISLANDS
Hagemeister I
Cape Newenham
Cape Constantine

SEMIDI ISLANDS
TRINITY ISLANDS
Chirikof I

134

Snowy owls nest on Alaska's tundra, in dry areas or on rocky ledges or cliffs.

ALASKA DIVISION OF TOURISM, ROBERT ANGELL

Bethel on the Kuskokwim River is the largest city in the area. It is a port for ocean ships. It is also the business and service center for surrounding villages. Besides following subsistence, its people work in private industries, for Native corporations, and for the government.

Most of the Yukon-Kuskokwim lowlands are wandering rivers, lakes, and wet tundra. Silt has been brought down by the Yukon and Kuskokwim Rivers.

These wetlands have been put aside as the largest wildlife refuge in the United States. It is called the Yukon Delta National Wildlife Refuge. However, people can still use the area for subsistence activities. Geese, swans, and ducks nest here by the thousands. Nearby the snowy owl hunts for small game.

From Bethel you fly southeast across the mountains to Dillingham, then Naknek. These two towns face Bristol Bay, one of the most important salmon fishing areas in the world. Both towns are centers for commercial fishing, but many people live by subsistence, too.

Many other birds nest in the wet Yukon-Kuskokwim lowlands.

STEVEN SEILLER

A Dangerous Job

ALASKA SEAFOOD MARKETING INSTITUTE

Most people know that ocean fishing can be dangerous, especially if the weather is bad. Perhaps no work is more scary than the crab fishery.

Suppose you were part of a crew on a crab boat fishing off Kodiak Island. You have to go out in the fall and winter when the crabs are just right for harvest. Of course, that's the very worst time of year for cold and storms. Daylight is short then, too. On this snowy day,

your 75-foot *Lady Jane* pitches and bucks in the wild sea. The *Lady* is coated with ice, and the captain fears she might roll over.

You slide the wheelhouse door open. A 50-knot wind blasts your face. The salty smell is always with you. You force your eyes open. You haven't slept for 18 hours. Every day the past week has been like that.

Water washes the deck, building a many layered skating rink outside. Stepping out,

JIM NILSEN

you grab a nearby steel ladder to keep from sliding overboard. The wind tears at you. You have gloves on, but already your hands are numbing.

Overhead the seven-foot-square steel mesh crab pot swings from a cable attached to a pulley. Its icy, dripping load of crab weighs a ton. If the cable breaks, you're gone.

The pot's lowered to the deck, and you and the crew empty it, hand over hand. You fight the rolling ship, the tearing wind. You have to work fast so the pot can go overboard to fish again.

Once the pot's empty, it's your turn for the job you hate most: rebaiting the pot. Someone hands you the fresh bait can. For the briefest moment you hesitate, but then you crawl into the pot. You remember the stories of heavy pots breaking loose, rolling off deck, and plunging to the bottom of the sea. The crew member inside was lost forever. Lost in the death cage.

You pull out the old bait can and put in the new. Then quickly you crawl back out of the pot. The pot is lifted and swung over the side. There's no time for relief, though. Here comes another dripping pot, swinging overhead. The process starts all over again.

Inland is lake country, and Alaska's largest lake, Iliamna. Alaskans and visitors go there to hunting and fishing lodges to enjoy the wilderness.

6 Alaska's Largest Island

From Bristol Bay you fly to Kodiak Island, home of giant brown bears and perhaps the world's best crab fishing. Some people there raise beef cattle. The first permanent Russian settlement in Alaska was on Kodiak Island.

Kodiak is the largest town in the Western Region. It has 6,400 people. That's about half of the 14,000 residents of Kodiak Island. Because of its location, it is an important center for commercial fishing and for shipping goods to the Aleutian Islands and the Alaska Peninsula.

ALASKA DIVISION OF TOURISM, ERNEST SCHNEIDER

Raising cattle is a successful industry on Kodiak Island.

Rivers winding through volcanic terrain create a "moonscape" in Katmai National Park and Preserve.

JÜRGEN KIENLE

7 Disasters and Rescues

Nearly 100 years ago, Kodiak and the Alaska Peninsula had their own disaster. In 1912, a volcano exploded in Katmai on the mainland across Shelikof Strait from Kodiak. At that time there was so much ash in the air, people could not breathe. The ash brought darkness for two days.

People were taken from the town to safety by a revenue cutter. Sailors on board had a hard time keeping ash from their burning eyes while

U. S. COAST GUARD

Each year the Coast Guard saves many lives and helps thousands of people in Alaskan waters.

shoveling it off the deck. Kodiak rivers were filled with ash. Birds, animals, and fish died.

It's odd, though. For all the destruction on Kodiak, the ash eventually nourished the land. A couple of years later, grasses and berries grew better in some places than ever before.

Today the U.S. Coast Guard is still active on Kodiak Island. Kodiak Search and Rescue units cover an area half the size of all the Lower 48 states. With so many Alaskans depending on water and air for travel or making their living, the Coast Guard is essential. The Coast Guard headed the rescue of more than 500 tourists when the cruise ship *Prinsendam* went down in the Gulf of Alaska in October of 1980.

8   The Alaska Peninsula

You've had a rest now, so step into your bush plane again and hop westward to the Alaska Peninsula. Lower altitude and drop down to Egegik on Bristol Bay.

McNeil River State Game Sanctuary on the Alaska Peninsula is carefully managed by the Alaska Department of Fish and Game. Visitors can study and photograph brown bears without endangering either themselves or the bears.

ALASKA DIVISION OF TOURISM

Fun in King Cove

People like living in the Western Region for many reasons. Here is what some students from King Cove have to say:

1. In sum - mer we have good weath - er. We ride our bikes a - round and
3. And some times we go wad - ing or swimming in the lakes but

when we go on pic - nics we bring a - long our hound.
if we see a bear there then we slam on the brakes.

2. We have fun in the sum - mer. We play all day out - side hunt - ing, pick - ing
4. We like to eat piz - za or may - be bar - be - que and some times we just

ber - ries, or fish - ing in the tide. King Cove is a fun place. The
hang around be - cause the sky is blue.

best is in the summer but when the wind blows in our face it can be a

bummer. Still we would - n't trade it 'cause no place could be fun ner.

Witten by Michelle Massion's third grade and Pop Wagner, Artist-in-Residence, King Cove School.

NATIONAL MARINE FISHERIES SERVICE

When people are careless with their garbage, fur seals and other animals suffer.

Because so much of the sea floor in Bristol Bay is continental shelf, fish and sea mammals find a wealth of food, and they come in great numbers. Fishermen and women come too, as well as people who process their catch.

To get an idea of how the fishing season affects Egegik, think of this. In winter about 170 people live there. During the commercial fishing season, however, there may be anywhere from 3,000 to 5,000 people! It is hard to imagine the changes that happen in town from February to July and then on to November.

9 The Aleutian Islands

Bank south and west now with your bush plane to the Aleutian Islands. The weather doesn't look too good, but you make it through.

ALASKA DIVISION OF TOURISM, ERNEST SCHNEIDER

Unalaska was the Number 1 fishing port in the United States in 1999.

Glide on a map with your finger across this amazing chain of small islands. They stretch 1,400 miles into the ocean. They have more than 50 volcanoes, 22 kinds of sea mammals in surrounding waters, and more than 230 kinds of birds. They also have earthquakes, tsunamis, and some of the stormiest weather in the world. Yet some people still like to live there!

Once Aleut people lived on nearly every island. Their descendants still live in the area today.

At the east end of the islands is Unalaska, the largest town in the Aleutians. People say Unalaska is where king crab is really the king.

Unalaska and its port of Dutch Harbor was the top fishing port in the United States in 1994. Five canneries on shore process halibut, cod, sablefish, salmon, pollock, and crab.

The Aleutian Islands must be one of the most remote places in the United States. Because of

The Aleutian Islands are remote and beautiful.

JÜRGEN KIENLE

In a tradition that is centuries old, Native people on St. Paul Island in the Pribilofs collect murre eggs for food. The seabirds nest in colonies on cliff ledges and on the flat tops of cliffs.

AMNWR, SEBERT

Because of their special character, much of the Aleutian Chain and its animals are protected as the Alaska Maritime National Wildlife Refuge.

10 Coming Back Home

There's lots more to see in Western Alaska, but your bush plane trip must come to an end. Though you've had only a whirlwind tour, you can see the Western Region has just about everything—ancient history, different cultures, all kinds of weather, animals and plants, big and small towns, mountains, volcanoes, hot springs, tundra, ice floes, wetlands, islands, peninsulas, rivers, lakes, and miles of seacoast.

11 A Mix of Lifestyles

More than 72,000 people live in the Western Region. That's about one out of every eight people living in Alaska. This area includes a greater percentage of Native people than any other region of the state.

As in all regions of Alaska, life in the Western Region combines old and new ways. Subsistence fishing, hunting, trapping, and gathering are followed here, too. Modern technology is added to it, making life easier. Most people use outboard motors, all-terrain vehicles, and snowmachines. Elementary students practice school work on computers. People may tell traditional stories on long winter evenings, but they also play bingo and cheer loudly at basketball games.

What seems most important to people in the Western Region is their connection to the land. One Yupik woman described what that meant for her. She had been raised in Bethel, went to college in the Lower 48 states, and worked "Outside" for 13 years. In the end, she returned to Alaska. She said:

> *Regardless of where I was or what I did, I knew that I belonged to some place back here …*
>
> *Last summer we went berry picking and camping near old Chevak. It's a powerful experience just to know that your ancestors lived in that area for thousands of years. Even though I'm supposed to be educated, even though I know the scientific method, I still feel their spirits.*

From "Hunters of the Lost Spirit," *National Geographic*, February 1983

Life in the Western Region combines old and new ways.

BERT NEIMEYER

Suggested Reading

Dieter, Betz. *The Bear Family.* N.Y.: Tambourine Books, 1991.

Lives of a grizzly bear family on a game reserve on the McNeil River in Alaska.

Hoyt-Goldsmith, Diane. *Arctic Hunter.* N.Y.: Holiday House, 1992.

A 10-year-old Inupiaq Eskimo boy living far north of the Arctic Circle describes a family trip to camp where he spends weeks hunting and fishing for food, and enjoys traditions.

O'Dell, Scott. *Black Star, Bright Dawn.* Boston: Houghton Mifflin, 1988.

Bright Dawn must face the challenge of the Iditarod dog sled race alone when her father is injured.

Scott, Jack Denton. *The Fur Seals of Pribilof.* N.Y.: G.P. Putnam's Sons, 1983.

Describes the life and habits of the fur seals.

AMNWR

The Interior Region

Young students going to school in the Interior might need a lot of closet space for a variety of clothing. Nowhere in Alaska is the weather more extreme.

1 Where Is It?

The Interior Region is just what it's called—the middle, or "inside" of Alaska. It is the side of the head where the ear would be on the Alaska mammoth pictured in your mind. Canada is the neighbor to the east. To the west is the Western Region along the Bering Sea coast. The Brooks Range separates the Interior from the Far North. The jagged Alaska Range marks the southern edge of the region. In between the mountain ranges lie more than 300 miles of wide valleys, lowlands, and plateaus. This is Interior Alaska.

ALASKA GATEWAY SCHOOL DISTRICT

Walter Northway School, Northway

Walter Northway

JOEL BENNETT

Chief Walter Northway was an Athabaskan leader who lived for 117 years. During that time he was an inspiration to young and old. The school in Northway honors his name and his ideals.

2 Weather Extremes

Weather in the Interior is different from weather in the Far North. Students who live inland need several different kinds of clothes.

JOHN TUCKEY

Mt. McKinley, the highest point in North America, is in Interior Alaska.

People in the Interior don't let cold weather stop their fun.

STEVEN SEILLER

They wear everything from heavy parkas for very cold weather, to swimming suits for very hot weather.

The Interior can be dusty or muddy, windy or calm. It might be foggy or clear, deathly cold or terribly hot. It can be brilliantly beautiful. On crisp winter nights people in the Interior may see the most magnificent displays of Northern Lights in the world.

The winter in Interior Alaska is very cold. However, people of the Interior don't let the cold stop them from their activities. Students still walk to school. People drive to work. Animals move around outside in their search for food.

Since it is so cold, sometimes special care is needed. People wear heavier clothes, for one thing. Car engines are plugged into heaters to keep them from freezing. Animals grow thicker fur.

Hot weather is the other extreme in the Interior. It comes during the long summer days. The record high temperature for Alaska is 100°F in 1915 at Fort Yukon. Now think of this: Fort Yukon is only eight miles from the **Arctic** Circle!

The reason for these weather extremes is that the Interior is far from the ocean. It is also shielded by mountains. There is nothing to make the winters milder and the summers cooler.

3 What Is There?

To the north and south, mountains rim the Interior Region, and these are **mountains!** The northern side of the Alaska Range builds and builds to the highest peak on the North American continent—Mt. McKinley. The mountain, which some people call Denali, "The Great One," was named for a U.S. President, William McKinley

ALASKA DEPARTMENT OF FISH & GAME, JOHN HYDE

The willow ptarmigan, Alaska's state bird, grows tufts of feathers between its toes to make its own winter "snowshoes." In summer, its mottled brown feathers blend into the colors of the landscape.

Birch trees are both useful and beautiful to Alaskans of the Interior Region. Kesler Woodward, an artist who lives in Fairbanks, has made more than 100 paintings of birches.

KESLER WOODWARD

(1843-1901). The mountain's peak reaches 20,320 feet into the sky. Mountain climbers from all over the world want to conquer that peak. In Denali National Park surrounding Mt. McKinley, animals and birds find safety, and people enjoy miles of wilderness.

Most of the Interior Region is low, rolling hills and flatlands. In its **boreal forests** spruce, birch, and aspen trees grow. Because of cold weather and patches of permafrost, the trees in most areas tend to be short and thin. They do not fill out and grow tall like trees in the coastal forests. In river valleys, where conditions are better, the trees grow bigger. The trees in both areas shelter lynx, snowshoe hares, and summer birds.

Upland and mountain areas are alpine, or higher, tundra. During the growing season, cranberries and blueberries dot the hillsides. From there you are likely to see caribou migrating through the territory. Near the mountains, golden eagles soar.

Sheltered from ocean moisture by the mountains, the Interior receives little rainfall. The heat of very long, sunny days takes moisture from trees and land. Everything gets very dry. Should a bolt of lightning streak to earth, or a careless human drop a match, **Swoosh!** the forest is aflame. Raging wildfires race through acres of timber, wiping out plants and sometimes animals. The destruction is not all bad, however. Over a period of time, the growth of new plants creates good food for moose, ptarmigan, and other animals.

BLM ALASKA FIRE SERVICE

In summer, many Alaskans work fighting wildfires. Fires in Interior Alaska may burn as much as a million acres each summer.

4   River "Highways"

Perhaps the most spectacular features of the Interior Region are its rivers. In summer these waterways teem with salmon. Small rivers and streams have whitefish, sheefish, and grayling. People in boats travel the rivers fishing, setting up fish camps, going to gather berries, or heading to town to pick up supplies.

Rivers are important highways in Interior Alaska.

In winter the rivers freeze over. Then people travel along these roads on snowmachines. Come spring, the ice breakup often causes brief flooding in river villages such as Fort Yukon.

The mighty Yukon is the longest river of the Interior. It wanders clear across the region in a broad arch. When the river floods in spring, water spreads over 200 miles of Yukon Flats. Then this

U.S. FISH & WILDLIFE SERVICE

Northern Lights, an oil painting by Sydney Laurence (1865-1940), one of Alaska's foremost landscape painters.

NATIONAL BANK OF ALASKA'S HERITAGE LIBRARY MUSEUM

Winter "Rainbow"—the Northern Lights

Few of nature's displays compare with the Northern Lights. These lights stream across the winter sky in colors of green, yellow, white, and red.

Early peoples of the world did not know what the lights were. Ancient Romans called them Aurora Borealis—"Aurora," after the goddess of Dawn, and "Boreas," after a Greek god of the "north wind."

Some people thought the lights were heavenly fires. Others thought they were dancing human spirits. Most people thought they were good, or at least that they did no harm. Some people today think they can hear the Northern Lights crackle.

No one knew what caused the lights. Only in the Twentieth Century did scientists find answers. They decided the lights were caused mostly by the electricity in solar winds and by the earth's magnetism at the North and South Poles.

Eventually, scientists figured out the Northern Lights could weave lengthwise across the sky for thousands of miles. They could also stretch anywhere from 50 to 600 miles high.

How powerful is the electrical energy in an aurora display? The lights that show in one night—that's ONE night—are estimated to contain three times the electrical energy used by all the people in the United States **for an entire year.**

Wow!

wetlands area makes perfect nesting grounds for migrating ducks and other waterfowl to raise their families.

Branching through the Interior are other rivers: the Porcupine, the Chandalar, the Tanana, the Chena, the Nenana, the Koyukuk, and the long Kuskokwim.

The Athabaskan Indians of Interior Alaska have been using these rivers for centuries. Today, too, water highways transport people, feed people, clean people, bring supplies to people, entertain people. The rivers carry soil, change the landscape, and make food and homes for animals and birds. For Interior Alaska, rivers are a network, like the arteries of life.

ALASKA DEPT. OF FISH & GAME, JOHN HYDE

Many Athabaskan families spend their summers at fish camp, gathering a year's supply of salmon.

5 The Interior's Other Highways

Interior Alaska has other networks, too. It has more roads and highway links than any other part of the state.

The Alaska Highway—the one built during World War II—enters Alaska from Canada and the Lower 48 states near Northway. The Parks Highway connects Fairbanks with Anchorage and makes a road link to Denali National Park. The Glenn, Richardson, and Tok Cutoff Highways tie the two roads together. These roadways complete a network of highways across the Interior and neighboring Southcentral Alaska.

The Usibelli Mine is about 100 miles south of Fairbanks. In 1992, the mine produced 1.5 million tons of coal. About half of it was used in Alaska. About half was exported to Korea.

ROGER W. PEARSON

ALASKA DIVISION OF TOURISM, ERNEST SCHNEIDER

Most tourists who come to Alaska visit Denali National Park. The Alaska Railroad can take them right into the park.

Fairbanks, main supply center for the Interior Region, and Alaska's second largest city.

Smaller roads lead off these highways to towns and villages. People have settled along the roadways, much as earlier people did along the rivers.

The Alaska Railroad is another connecting link. It runs south from Fairbanks to Anchorage, and then to Whittier and Seward on the Kenai Peninsula. At Nenana the railroad connects with river barges to ship goods to villages along the Yukon River. In summer, the railroad carries thousands of tourists to Denali National Park.

The number of tourists who visit Denali Park during a year might surprise you. In 1942 there were only 100 visitors. In 2000, there were 364,000! That's more than half the total population of Alaska in 2000. And they all come because of this very important feature of Alaska's geography.

6 Alaska's Second Largest City

About 98,000 people now live in Interior Alaska. Most of them, about 83,000, live in or near the city of Fairbanks. More than 15,000 other Alaskans live in towns, villages, and rural

ALASKA DIVISION OF TOURISM

homes throughout the Interior. A number of villages are the traditional homes of Alaska's Athabaskan Indian people.

Fairbanks is by far the largest city in the Interior. It is the second largest city in Alaska. If you poked your finger right at the center of the state, Fairbanks would be a little to the east, toward Canada. The town was named after Charles Fairbanks (1852-1918), who became vice president of the United States.

In 1902 shouts of **Gold!** brought people to the area where Fairbanks would be in 1903. It was then Felix Pedro (1860?-1910) struck it rich near the Tanana River.

The town grew as the supply center for the Interior. A hospital and schools were built, and families settled in.

With so many people coming to Fairbanks, more food and supplies were needed. Many families grew their own gardens during the long summer days. The U.S. government helped by building an experimental farm close by to see what plants would grow best in Alaska. Eventually this farm, along with classes in minerals for miners, developed into a college. Next, it became the University of Alaska.

Today, the Tanana Valley near Fairbanks and Delta Junction is one of Alaska's best farming areas. The part of the valley near Fairbanks produces mostly hay and vegetable crops such

MARIE ANGAIAK

The University of Alaska Experimental Farm still studies how crops and animals can thrive in Alaska. Students from University Park Elementary School visited the farm on a class trip.

High school students from all around Alaska attend Space Camp and visit the University's Poker Flats Research Range.

UAF PHOTO BY CALVIN P. WHITE

People enjoy outdoor sports on Chena Lakes near Fairbanks.

CALVIN P. WHITE

as potatoes, cabbage, lettuce, and cucumbers. The part of the valley near Delta Junction grows barley and hay and even has a big dairy. Bison were brought into the Delta area in the 1920s.

Fairbanks was linked to the Alaska Railroad in 1923. The railroad and small branch railways transported coal and other minerals from Interior areas. As air transportation grew, Fairbanks became connected with other towns in a matter of hours. The first airport in Alaska was built in Fairbanks in the early 1920s.

A couple of years before the Alaska Highway was built during World War II, a military base, Ladd Field, was constructed in Fairbanks. All this building activity brought in more people.

The town grew again when development of the Prudhoe Bay oil fields caused a flood of people north in the 1970s. The TransAlaska Pipeline passes close to Fairbanks on its journey south.

Today, there are people in Fairbanks from many cultures and backgrounds. Most people work for the University, government, the military, or in service jobs.

Students in a fourth grade class at Nordale Elementary School in Fairbanks tell of their town's resources and the movements of its people:

The resources we export are knowledge, Native arts and furs. These resources go all around the world.

Some of the things we import are lobsters from Maine, potatoes from Idaho, pineapples from Hawaii, and money from Washington, D.C.

People move to Fairbanks because of being in the military, to be with their families, because they get jobs, and because they like the weather.

People leave Fairbanks because it's too cold, their family leaves, the weather is bad, or they are transferred from jobs.

Ji Chang, Richie Schloesser, Brad Farrell, Lauren Rao.
Nordale Elementary, Fairbanks. Teacher Jill Addington

ALASKA DIVISION OF TOURISM

The knuckle hop is a major event at the World Eskimo Indian Olympics in Fairbanks each year. Many events promote skills important to hunting or survival in the North.

7   Weather Problems

People may go along in their work and play, but in the end, nature still rules. Because of where they are located, Fairbanks and its surrounding area have some special problems.

Nature got the attention of everyone in Fairbanks in August of 1967. During that summer, more rain than usual fell in the area. The two rivers close by, the Chena and the Tanana, could not handle all the water. The Chena overflowed, and ground partially filled with permafrost could not soak up the water. Flood waters in Fairbanks and the town of Nenana were nine feet deep in some areas. What a mess of mud and water there was in buildings and in the streets! Most people left town or took shelter on high ground near the University of Alaska. The worst part is that five people died.

The Chena River Lakes Project was built to prevent flood damage in the Fairbanks area.

U.S. ARMY CORPS OF ENGINEERS

Ice fog can make driving difficult during cold weather in Fairbanks.

ROGER W. PEARSON

Farmers use modern equipment in the Tanana Valley near Delta Junction. Most farmers there grow barley and hay. There is also a large bison herd.

ALASKA DIVISION OF TOURISM

After that disaster, the U.S. Army built a dam near Fairbanks called the Chena River Lakes Flood Control Project. This dam can hold extra water and move it elsewhere so flooding will not occur again.

Another special problem facing Fairbanks and the Interior is ice fog. You need two things to make ice fog. You need very cold weather (around minus 25°F or lower) and warmer water vapor meeting this cooled air. The water vapor freezes into tiny ice crystals that hang in the air. If many ice crystals fill the air, they form a kind of fog.

If the moisture rises from hot springs or open rivers, the ice fog is not harmful. But if the moisture comes from car exhausts or building heating units, the ice crystals form around pollution particles. They hold harmful substances in the air that people breathe. Ice fog also makes it difficult for people to see where they are going when they are driving.

8   Rural Villages

Fairbanks has the most people, but there are many other towns and villages in the Interior Region. More than 6,000 people residing outside the Fairbanks area are Athabaskan Indians. Since the early days, these people have lived along the rivers. The location of many villages still reflects that history.

In some places, when trading posts or mines were built, people settled near them. Villages grew. People settled along the highways, too, or at special places such as hot springs, or where the Alaska Railroad had a stop.

Many Native activities in the Interior Region take place under Doyon, Limited. This is one of the 12 regional corporations created under the Alaska Native Claims Settlement Act of 1971. Among many other projects, Doyon is involved in North Slope oil drilling, providing food and supplies for the workers, and security.

Subsistence activities such as hunting, fishing, gathering, and trapping, are very important to rural Alaskans in the Interior. Among people of Athabaskan heritage, Native traditions are strong. Among newcomers there is great pride in living well, close to the land.

Today rural villages in the Interior are a mix of old and new. Besides smokehouses and caches,

STEVEN SEILLER

Songs, dances, and games are a part of potlatch celebrations in villages such as Minto in Interior Alaska.

HARVEY BRANDT

Gold mining has a long, colorful history in Interior Alaska. Polar Mining still produces gold a few miles northwest of Fairbanks.

ALASKA DEPARTMENT OF FISH & GAME, JOHN HYDE

The thick, deep brown pelts of beaver brought the earliest trappers and traders to Alaska. Today the pelts are still prized for making cold weather coats and hats.

most have a community electric generator, satellite telephones, a health clinic, and television and videos. Snowmachines have replaced most sled dogs. Chain saws, as well as axes, are used for cutting wood. Moose or caribou meat from the wild is set on the family table along with fresh vegetables and canned soda pop from the village store.

Athabaskan Edwin Simon (1898-1979) lived at Huslia on the Koyukuk River. Before his death he told what he liked about life in his rural village. He said:

> *Compared to Cutoff, this Huslia is better country. Lot of fish and lot of game. High ground. Used to be lot of muskrats and lots of beaver. More slough and more fish around. You can go out and put a fishnet anyplace and catch all kinds of fish. That why it's good country to live.*

From *Edwin Simon, Huslia: A Biography.*

Suggested Reading

Griese, Arnold. *Anna's Athabaskan Summer.* Honesdale, Pa.: Boyds Mills Press/ Distributed by St. Martin's Press, 1995.

> A young Athabaskan girl and her family make the annual return to their summer fish camp where they prepare for the long winter ahead.

Hill, Kirkpatrick. *Toughboy and Sister.* N.Y.: Puffin Books, 1990.

> The death of their father strands ten-year-old Toughboy and his younger sister at a remote fishing cabin in the Yukon, where they spend the summer trying to cope with dwindling food supplies and hostile wildlife. (Sequel—*Winter Camp.* McElderry Bks., 1993)

Rogers, Jean. *The Secret Moose.* N.Y.: Greenwillow Books, 1985.

> A young boy living in Alaska develops an interest in moose and their habits after he sees a moose in his backyard and decides to follow it.

Souza, Dorothy. *Northern Lights.* Minneapolis, Mn.: Carolrhoda Books, 1994.

> Discusses the origin, characteristics and lore of the Northern and Southern Lights known as *auroras.*

The Southcentral Region

Students who live in Southcentral Alaska are likely to need heavy clothing in winter and rain gear during the summer. Of course, that depends on where you live. Some parts of the region are not as rainy as others.

1 Where Is It?

The Southcentral Region is a half-moon shaped area located around the mouth and chin of the Alaska mammoth you have pictured in your mind. The Kenai Peninsula could easily be the mammoth's lower jaw. The region curves around the north side of the Gulf of Alaska. Southcentral borders on Canada to the east and a small portion of the Western Region to the west. The Alaska Range separates Southcentral from the Interior Region to the north. More Alaskans live in Southcentral than in any other region of the state.

Gladys Wood

One of the elementary schools in Alaska's largest city is named for Gladys Leona Foster Wood. As a teacher, principal, and educational leader, Mrs. Wood dedicated 20 years to the young people of Anchorage.

Students outside Gladys Wood Elementary School, Anchorage

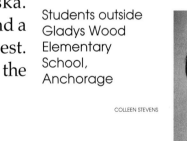

COLLEEN STEVENS

2 What Is There?

The mountains of the Alaska Range form the region's northern border. They hold out the really cold

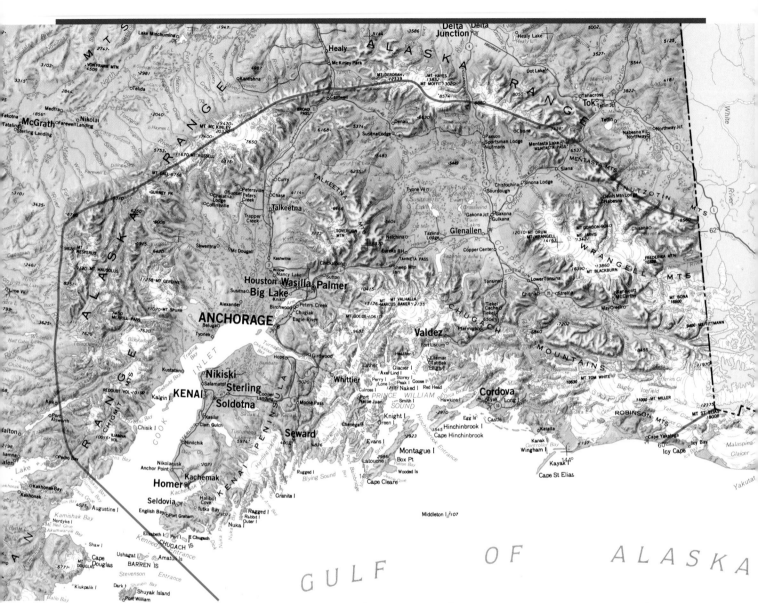

weather from the Interior Region and hold in warm, moist air from the ocean. You know these mountains are high since they are the southern side of Mt. McKinley and its cousin peaks.

Lower mountain ranges to the east—the Kenai and the Chugach—protect the Cook Inlet area from Gulf storms. Between the Alaska Range and these lower ranges lie Cook Inlet and the Matanuska and Susitna river valleys.

The mild, wet weather of Southcentral encourages the growth of hemlock, spruce, birch, and aspen trees on mountain slopes and in valleys. Dall sheep, mountain goats, and bears roam the higher elevations. Red foxes and beavers like the lowlands. Moose range high and low according to the season.

Much of Southcentral Alaska is seacoast along the Gulf of Alaska. Looking at a map, follow along from left to right.

To the southwest, Cook Inlet separates the Kenai Peninsula from the mainland. To the center is Prince William Sound. To the east the Wrangell Mountains stretch south along the glacier-backed coast. The Wrangells meet the St. Elias Mountains near Icy Bay. Offshore are fish, seals, sea otters, and whales. Overhead fly sea birds that live along the coast.

ALASKA DIVISION OF TOURISM

Moose are the largest members of the deer family, and Alaska's moose are the biggest in the world. They are an important source of food for Alaskans. Visitors also come from throughout the world to hunt, photograph, or just watch them.

The focal point of ocean travel to Southcentral Alaska is through Cook Inlet. The inlet is more than 200 miles long. If you see it on a map, this inlet looks like other bodies of water. But the waters of Cook Inlet can be tricky.

First, there are rivers flowing into upper Cook Inlet. That sends water currents one way. Next the rising and falling of tides twice a day causes another water flow. High tide here is really high (maybe 30 feet or more at Anchorage). Then there is ice on the water four months a year. The ice is broken by tidal action. Besides those water actions, fingers of land force water currents this way or that.

To sum it up, upper Cook Inlet waters are confusing and swirling and fast. Big ships can handle all these water forces, but it is no place for sport fishing or kayaking.

This Cook Inlet passage is a wide finger of water that points directly to the largest city in Alaska—Anchorage.

3 Alaska's Largest City

The city's name, Anchorage, tells its beginnings. It was a place where boats anchored years ago. It is the only older city in Alaska that was not started because of mining, fishing, or some other natural resource. Today it is Alaska's largest port.

It is believed that Eskimo people first lived in the Cook Inlet Basin about 2,000 years ago. Remains of their culture and life have been found by people today digging in ancient trash dumps, or *middens*. Athabaskan Indians settled there later. Descendants of both groups still live in the area.

Anchorage began as a port city and the headquarters for the

Anchorage, Alaska's largest city, is sheltered and made beautiful by the Chugach Mountains.

JIM HAUCK

Alaska Railroad. Construction on the railroad started in 1915. The line was built to transport coal and other minerals from the Interior to Seward, an ice-free ocean port. People hurried north from the United States to work on the railroad. After that, the city grew steadily due mostly to increased transportation and communications.

When World War II began, the federal government built military bases in Anchorage. The town was the supply point for other places in Alaska. Military people came, and some stayed on after the war.

In 1957 an oil company discovered oil on the Kenai Peninsula to the south, then later in Cook Inlet. As more people arrived, Anchorage became the headquarters for oil companies drilling in Alaska.

Today people work at a variety of jobs in Anchorage. The military is a big employer. Many people work in transportation or communications. Government agencies employ people, as do construction companies, hospitals, stores, schools, restaurants, and small businesses. In recent years, tourism has grown tremendously.

Inside the Municipality of Anchorage alone, you will find about 41 percent of all Alaskans. That's about 260,000 people. If you include people in the Southcentral Region outside the city, 60 percent of all Alaskans live there. That's more than half the people in the entire state!

JOHN TUCKEY

Almost 80 percent of all the cargo coming into Alaska goes through the Port of Anchorage. In 1994, the port handled 2.7 million tons of cargo.

In Anchorage both visitors and residents can enjoy biking along beautiful Turnagain Arm.

ALASKA DIVISION OF TOURISM, ERNEST SCHNEIDER

ANCHORAGE CONVENTION & VISITORS BUREAU, GRANT KLOTZ

Kids get to race on snowshoes during Anchorage's annual Fur Rondezvous.

Of course all those people are not just adults. There are more students in Anchorage than in any other region of the state, too. In Anchorage alone, 27,000 elementary students attend school. That's almost the number of all the people in Juneau, the capital of Alaska.

Why do so many people live in the Anchorage area?

For one reason, though the Gulf of Alaska whips up terrible storms, its waters never freeze over as more northerly waters do. Ships can come and go all year round. The biggest Alaskan city is protected from Gulf storms by the mountains surrounding it.

The weather in Anchorage is less extreme than in the Far North or Interior Regions. Summer temperatures range around 60°F. Winter temperatures are usually just above 0°F. There is not as much rain as in Southeast Alaska to the south.

Another reason Anchorage has grown is that it is centrally located. The city is like the hub of a wheel. It is the center for shipping supplies and moving people to northern and western Alaska. The Alaska Railroad travels through Anchorage, going north to Fairbanks or south to Seward.

Anchorage is also one corner of Alaska's great network of highways. One branch of the Alaska

Highway connects the city with Canada and the continental United States. From Anchorage, highways radiate out to towns such as Willow, Soldotna, Kenai, Valdez, and Palmer. The Parks Highway heads north to Denali National Park and on to Fairbanks.

The Anchorage Airport is a central point for jets traveling to Asia and Europe. Flights from the Lower 48 states stop there to make connections for travel north.

Many Alaskans travel to Anchorage for business, shopping, school events, or doctor and dentist appointments. They travel on airlines with small commuter planes or planes on floats or skis. Landing areas serve residents and tourists coming north to hunt or fish. In fact, Anchorage has the largest floatplane base in the **world**.

Another reason Anchorage has grown is that the country around it is beautiful and varied. People can ski at Alyeska Ski Resort. Hunters can hunt big game in the mountains. People can sport fish in Kenai Peninsula lakes and rivers, or hike among the hills. With a railroad, waterways, highways, and airways, it is easy to get around. People can enjoy the convenience of big city life, while the peace of the wilderness is a short distance away.

ALASKA DIVISION OF TOURISM

Anchorage is the largest U.S. city located near the polar air routes. Its International Airport is a major stop for planes carrying cargo between Europe and Asia and between Asia and North America.

JOHN TUCKEY

The Canine Connection

"Mushing" is Alaska's state sport.

Perhaps no animal has done more for Alaska's development than the dog. Certainly it has been important. Northern breeds probably developed from the wolf.

Scientists digging for artifacts found that dogs must have pulled sleds in Alaska at least 300 years ago. Use of dog sleds allowed early Alaskans to range farther in hunting, and to bring heavy loads back home.

Since those years, dogs have been used in Alaska to carry supplies and mail. They have run traplines, freighted mining equipment, towed boats, guarded people and places, saved lives, helped string telephone wire, and herded reindeer. They have also been used in search and rescue work, racing, patrolling, and military operations. Some dogs were companions and pets. Only since the airplane and the snowmachine has the need for work dogs declined.

Today, numerous dogs are raised especially for racing with sleds, or "dog mushing." Mushing is Alaska's official state sport. The best known Alaska race is the world-famous Iditarod. Mushers start in Anchorage and run 1,000 miles to Nome. Besides the terribly long distance, the race holds dangers from very cold weather, holes in river ice, unmarked parts of the trail, exhaustion, or injuries for both dogs and mushers. Yet every year people take the challenge. Most Alaskans know the names of Leonhard Seppala, Joe Redington, Sr., Susan Butcher, George Attla, Libby Riddles, and Joseph Romig—all mushers who stand out in Alaska dog racing history.

Races such as the Iditarod, the Yukon Quest, and the World Championship Sled Dog Race in Anchorage attract thousands of dog race fans and tourists. Many small towns and villages have their own mushing events, too. The dog—the racing sled dog—makes it all possible.

JIM HAUCK

4 The Matanuska and Susitna Valleys

Some people outside Alaska still think Alaska is mostly snow and cold. They might say, "Sure, you have polar bears and glaciers, but you can't grow any food up there. Not with all that snow and ice."

They are wrong. Or at least partly wrong.

Alaska has never been known as a "garden spot" of the world, like California or Florida. Alaska does not ship oranges to Oregon or apples to New Zealand. Plus, it's true, temperatures are cold, and permafrost remains under a good share of northern soil. But remember, Alaska has something other places may not. It has long, bright growing days in the summer—days longer than in other parts of the United States.

Rimmed by mountains and lined by two great rivers, the Matanuska-Susitna ("Mat-Su") area is one of Alaska's rich farming regions. Some call it the "food basket" for Anchorage and nearby military bases. Hardy vegetables such as potatoes and cabbage grow to huge proportions. Hay flourishes there, and cows are raised to give milk.

Many people who work in Anchorage like to live in the Mat-Su Valley. Palmer and Wasilla are the major towns in the area. A fourth grader from

ALASKA DIVISION OF TOURISM

The Matanuska Valley near Anchorage is one of Alaska's richest farming regions.

Young people in the Matanuska and Susitna Valleys learn to raise high quality animals and produce. This is Harmony Reed of the Hatcher Pass Herders 4-H Club.

AL FLORY

167

Matanuska-Susitna Borough

Map by Brad Truett and Sean M. Finley,
Finger Lake Elementary, Palmer. Teacher Diana Anderson

Sherrod Elementary tells about Palmer in a poem:

Palmer

Giant veggies, good fishing, giant mushrooms
Rainy, cold, itchy
Winter gear and a warm place to stay
Car, money, house
Lots of money to come here and for coal
Tommy Moe and other people
Small city, air is cleaner, less people
Perfect home

Reuben Mayer, Sherrod Elementary, Palmer. Teacher Marti Wynn

The Mat-Su Valley is also a recreational area for Alaskan visitors. Besides kayaking, swimming, boating, and rafting, there are hunting and fishing. Students at Finger Lake Elementary School give a good idea of what you can do for fun.

Skiing and hiking are some good family activities. They are good activities if you are alone or with friends, too. There are lots of good trails to ski. There are some good trails to Colony High School and there's Hatcher Pass. There are lots of good places to hike. Crevasse Moraine is a good place to hike. So is Hatcher Pass. Hiking and skiing are some good things to do if you have free time.

Fishing and hunting are very fun things to do. Finger Lake is a pretty good place to go fishing. You can also see a lot of leeches, and little sea creatures. The fish are very little, though. In winter you can go moose hunting. In the summer you can go duck hunting and also go hunting for geese.

Alyson Lucier, Ingrid Backus, Jessica Cler, Finger Lake Elementary, Palmer. Teacher Diana Anderson

Let's take a short trip south now and look at the Kenai Peninsula.

5 The Kenai Peninsula

Mountains, hills, lowlands, glaciers, and rivers form the land of the Kenai Peninsula. It is washed by Cook Inlet on the west and Prince William Sound on the east.

A large portion of Alaska's population lives on the Kenai Peninsula, a next door neighbor to Anchorage. The Kenai Borough is the fourth largest in the state, with about 50,000 people. Towns such as Homer, Seward, Port Graham, and Kenai mark the coast.

The Seward Highway is the only road that runs from Anchorage to the peninsula. By plane, Kenai is 60 miles away. Being so close, the area is one of the "playgrounds" for Anchorage. People come to fish, hunt, ski, boat, and snowshoe during certain seasons. Birds and animals come, too. Hundreds of geese stop at Kenai on their migrating way north. Whales play in the water.

The Kenai Peninsula is the place where Alaskans work, too. A petroleum refinery at Nikiski supplies fuel for Alaskan homes and cars. Natural gas products from another plant are shipped to Asia. Ships at Seward carry coal from Usibelli Coal Mine to Korea. Forestry on the Kenai has been affected by the spruce bark beetle. These tiny insects burrow into spruce trees and cause serious problems.

NANCY RABENER

Recreation and industry are found side by side on the Kenai Peninsula. Tourists from around the world visit to enjoy the scenery.

Oil drilling takes place in offshore waters.

ALASKA DIVISION OF TOURISM

169

Kandi Sowards, Nona Myrick, Flo Widman, Hope Elementary, School. Teacher MaryCarol Nelson

Hope is a small community on the Kenai Peninsula.

The tourist industry employs many people on the Kenai. Sightseeing and fishing are the big draws. During the summer on Homer Spit, you can see huge halibut hanging on racks, caught by Alaskans and visitors. The world's largest king salmon, a 97-pounder, was caught in the Kenai River.

The Kenai Peninsula is so popular, there are problems. Some people feel too many people are fishing out the rivers and salt waters. Oil drilling and environmental problems arise. Kenai people want to have rules so the resources are not all used up.

6   Living in an Earthquake Zone

The area along the northern Gulf of Alaska coast sits on a *fault zone*, a very unstable part of the earth's crust. People will always remember the Friday before Easter, March 27, 1964. At that time, the area was hit by the hardest earthquake ever to shake the North American continent.

On that Friday, the weather was normal for March—in the 20s and 30s F. It was 5:36 in the evening. When the quake hit, the shaking and rolling of the earth was frightening! The jolts broke roads in half. Great slabs of earth dropped, tearing apart buildings, roads, railroad tracks, and

U.S. GEOLOGICAL SURVEY

bridges. The heaving of the earth snapped electric poles and water pipes. Worst of all, more than 100 people died.

Away from towns, mountains shook and glaciers jumped. A great tsunami washed away homes and some entire coastal towns. In harbors, boats were flung to land like wooden bowls. However, school students were lucky. Schools had been closed for the Easter holiday, and most kids were at home. In photographs, buildings of Government Hill Elementary School in Anchorage look like jumbled, broken boxes. If the quake had happened during school hours, no one likes to think of what could have happened.

Anchorage and other Southcentral communities have rebuilt since the earthquake more than 30 years ago. However, people know Southcentral still sits on a shaky part of the earth's crust. The Alaska Tsunami Warning Center in Palmer has been set up to watch for quakes and tsunamis in the future.

Government Hill School in Anchorage was devastated by the 1964 Good Friday Earthquake. Fortunately, no one was in the building during the quake.

When instruments at an earthquake monitoring station sense up-and-down or sideways ground motion, they send electrical signals that can be studied in great detail by scientists. The signals also can be picked up and recorded by a **helicorder,** an instrument with a pen attached to a paper-covered drum. As the drum turns, the pen wiggles, recording the ground's motion in a **seismogram.**

This recording is from the Alaska Earthquake Information Center at the Geophysical Institute, University of Alaska Fairbanks.

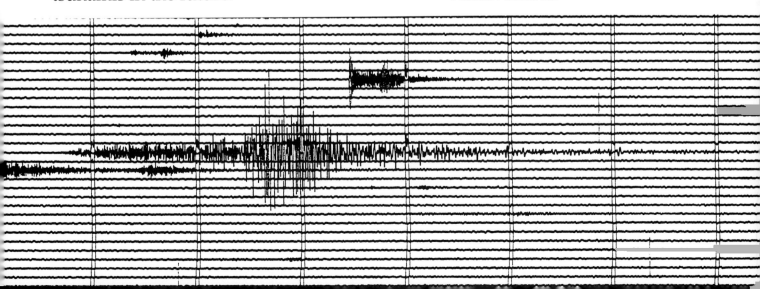

ANCHORAGE DAILY NEWS, JIM LAVRAKAS

Volcanic ash "fallout" in the air is harmful to engines and people's lungs. Here a man in Anchorage is helping a woman change the air filter in her car after Mt. Spurr erupted in August 1992.

People in Southcentral Alaska live and work close to volcanoes.

JIM NILSEN

7 Living Close to Volcanoes

Some of Alaska's volcanoes are in the Southcentral Region. This area is part of the "Rim of Fire," the shaky section of earth's crust you studied about earlier. Volcanic eruptions can cause serious problems once in a while.

When volcanic ash is thrown into the air, planes must be grounded. Travelers cannot go anywhere. The fine, soft dust can ruin engines and hurt people who breathe it.

Mt. Spurr is a mountain west of Anchorage. It had an ice-filled crater, and no one ever remembered it being anything but peaceful. In July of 1953 it violently erupted gases, cinders, steam, and ash, sending a mushroom-shaped cloud high into the sky. Anchorage was 80 miles away, but by noon heavy ash was falling on the city. The ash was so thick the air grew dark. The street light mechanism indicated **night,** and the street lights turned on automatically!

More recently, Mt. Augustine and Mt. Redoubt have erupted. Also, in 1992, Mt. Spurr erupted again and dumped ash over the Cook Inlet area.

8   Oil Spill in Prince William Sound

Not all problems in Southcentral Alaska are caused by nature. One of the worst disasters happened a few years ago. The oil spill that many people feared when the TransAlaska Pipeline was put in became a fact. The supertanker *Exxon Valdez* had an accident and spilled oil into Prince William Sound. It was another Good Friday, March 24, 1989.

AMNWR, A. SOWIS

AMNWR

Thousands of sea otters and birds died when oil from the water coated their fur or feathers. Hundreds of volunteers tried to capture oiled animals and clean them.

AMNWR, FOSTER

Photographs can show only a little bit about the total tragic effects of the oil spill. Probably no one will ever understand them all. Scientists know that more than 3,000 sea otters died the first few weeks. Thousands more died later, and so did thousands of birds. People will study long-term effects for years to come.

The oil had made it from Prudhoe Bay in the Arctic, through 800

Some oil floated on top of the water as a thick, gummy mousse.

AMNWR, A. SOWIS

miles of the pipeline, to Valdez. The tanker had loaded at the terminal there and left the dock, heading south. To avoid icebergs, the ship left the safe shipping lane it was supposed to follow. It hit Bligh Reef and ripped open its hull. The tanker spilled 11 million gallons of crude oil into Prince William Sound.

Oil does not dissolve, or blend with water and eventually disappear as salt does. It stays separate on the surface or in the water, or it sinks down and settles on the bottom. It has to be cleaned up. That is a difficult, if not impossible, job.

When oil was spilled in Prince William Sound, thousands of seabirds and sea animals died. Shellfish and other sea life died or were poisoned. Places on shore where land animals eat were coated with oil. Streams where salmon lay eggs were soaked with oil. Plants and animals throughout the food chain were affected.

Eventually the spill washed into Cook Inlet, all the way to Katmai National Park. The food supply of Native people who depend on subsistence was threatened. So was commercial fishing.

AMNWR, WILLIAMSON

Fishermen and other volunteers dragged huge booms around the oil. They tried to keep it from spreading, especially when it threatened nearby salmon hatcheries.

Cleaning beaches with hot water under pressure occupied thousands of people. Later, people debated whether this approach did more harm than good.

AMNWR, McWHORTER

AMNWR, KATHY HILL

A number of sea otters were cleaned and released back into the wild. No one knows how well they survived.

The oil company, state and federal workers, and private citizens tried to clean up the mess. The U.S. Coast Guard organized the work. It was a gigantic task. Every known method of cleaning was tried, from water hoses, to suction machines, to chemicals, to tractors, to paper towels. A rescue center was established in Valdez to try to save as many animals as possible.

People are still trying to understand how the spill may affect the animals, plants, and environment of Prince William Sound in the years to come.

Where did all that oil go?

Oil eventually reached shorelines 600 miles southwest of Bligh Reef, where the spill occurred.

Source: Alaska Department of Environmental Conservation

How much oil was spilled?

To get an idea of how much oil was spilled, think of this: If you left your kitchen faucet running at full volume all the time, it would take almost ten years to equal the amount of oil spilled.

Source: Pratt Museum, Homer

The Coast Guard coordinated cleanup efforts.

AMNWR

What's Best for Everyone?

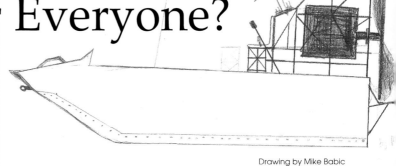

Drawing by Mike Babic

In today's world, people compete to use land and resources in different ways. Sometimes people disagree about what is good for people, animals, and the land. Here's an example:

Several fifth grade students from Mt. Eccles Elementary School in Cordova discuss a problem in their community. They give two sides to the question of having airboats on the Copper River Delta.

FOR: Mike Babic and Shawn Espejo

Airboats on the Copper River Delta help us keep a good healthy herd. For instance this year 97 percent of the bull moose east of the Copper River were harvested by airboats. If airboats are outlawed, the moose herd would grow too big and there wouldn't be enough food for the moose. Airboats are also used to transport meat, hunters, supplies for camps, and for just driving around.

People should allow the use of airboats because they do not pollute or give any fish wounds. They do not harm the environment.

AGAINST: Diane Schneider and Jessica Neale

We should not have airboats east of the Copper River Delta because they drive the moose into the woods. The airboats' loud engines scare the moose and they get frantic. Airboats also disturb the other wildlife because of pollution. The churning water and gasoline can affect the fish and birds.

Some people say that the airboats help keep the population of the moose down so they won't starve. Here in Cordova that is not a problem. We don't have too many moose! Our moose population needs to grow more before the airboats should be allowed to go onto the Delta.

GLENN JUDAY

There are always two or more sides to every question. Consider these issues, and see what you think.

Mt. Eccles Elementary School, Cordova.
Teacher Mary T. Armantrout

The Copper River delta

9 Towns and Rural Areas

Most towns in Southcentral Alaska cluster close to the coast. The sea provides jobs, transportation, food, and recreation. There are traditional Native villages and bustling fishing ports. In some villages people live by subsistence. In others, they are tied closely to the city by highways.

Not all the activity is along the coast, however. Away from the sea and surrounded by mountains is the Copper River Valley. Here the rivers and forests offer fishing, hunting, and trapping.

The long Copper River flows from the valley and forms a broad flatland as it drains into the Gulf of Alaska. Thousands of migrating birds use the delta for nesting, or as a rest stop on their way north. The river and its delta are also spawning

NANCY RABENER

The old Kennecott Copper Mine near McCarthy is now a tourist attraction. More than $200 million in copper and silver was taken from the mine before it closed in 1938. It was one of the world's richest copper finds.

Impossible Journey

Trapper Amos Fleury received a Christmas present in 1932—his life. The 11-year-old who gave it to him was an Ahtna Indian girl named Nena McKinley.

Amos fell through river ice near his lonely cabin on Klutina Lake. Nena was staying in a cabin nearby with her grandfather. The McKinleys found Amos. They knew he needed hospital care or he would die.

They had to have an airplane fly to Klutina Lake to pick up the injured man. But the closest phone connection to call a pilot was at Copper Center, 22 miles away. Nena's grandfather had to stay with the injured man. Nena was the only one left to make such an impossible journey.

The idea of all that distance did not stop Nena. She strapped on her snowshoes and took off. That 11-year-old girl tramped all night, in darkness, alone, in sub-zero weather, through dangerous areas, all 22 miles to Copper Center!

There the pilot was contacted. He flew to Klutina Lake, picked up the injured man, and took him to a hospital in Cordova.

Nena's trip saved Amos Fleury's life.

ALASKA DIVISION OF TOURISM

Seldovia is a small town across Kachemak Bay from Homer. It can be reached only by plane or boat.

Chris Chandler, Mt. Eccles Elementary, Cordova. Teacher Mary T. Armantrout

grounds for salmon and herring caught by fishermen in the Gulf and Prince William Sound.

The Wrangell and St. Elias Mountains spread across the eastern section of Southcentral. They stretch south in a wilderness of mountains and glaciers that extend into the Southeast Region.

The Wrangell Mountains have long held secret treasures of gold, copper, silver, and coal. Early in this century, tons of minerals were taken out by the Kennecott Copper Company mine until it closed in 1938.

More people live in Southcentral than in any other region. Southcentral, too, is the major center for business in the state. Yet the area has a variety of glaciers, coastline, and mountains where people can live and work in a wilderness setting as well.

Suggested Reading

Dixon, Ann. *The Sleeping Lady.* Seattle: Alaska Northwest Books, 1994.

> A modern-day folk tale of Alaska's first snowfall in the Cook Inlet village of the giant people.

Oberle, Joseph. *Anchorage.* Minneapolis, Mn.: Dillon Press, 1990.

> Introduces Anchorage, its history, neighborhoods, people, attractions, and festivals.

Pedersen, Elsa. *House Upon a Rock.* Chicago, Il: Adams Press, 1986.

> A young teenage boy and his family learn to live with problems caused by the Good Friday earthquake and tidal wave.

Rand, Gloria. *Prince William.* N.Y.: Henry Holt, 1992.

> A young girl rescues a baby seal hurt by the oil spill and watches it recover at a nearby animal hospital.

The Southeast Region

In the Southeast region, it might be a good idea to have a pair of rubber boots and rain gear close by. Because, students, there is rain! Everything from light misty rain to the hard, heavy, wet stuff.

Students in Port Alexander on Baranof Island have more than rain to think about. Some boys and girls live across the bay from school, and they take a "school boat" to get there. One teacher's aide used to paddle a kayak to school every day.

While students in other places wait on a street corner for the school bus, these students have to check the **tides**. By seeing whether the tide is in or out, boys and girls know where to stand for the school boat. If the bay is too rough to cross, students stay home and receive their school assignments by CB radio or telephone.

1 Where Is It?

The Southeast Region is the neck of the Alaska mammoth you have pictured in your mind.

J.R. Gildersleeve

Roger "J.R." Gildersleeve came to Alaska with his brother and built up Gildersleeve Logging Company near Ketchikan and Prince of Wales Island. Company employees and their families lived on a floating camp that moved, along with its school, church, and work buildings, wherever logging operations took place. J.R. helped start the Alaska Loggers Association and served two years as its president.

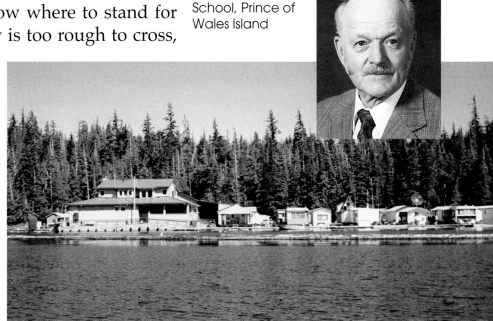

ALASKA FOREST ASSOCIATION

J.R. Gildersleeve School, Prince of Wales Island

SOUTHEAST ISLAND SCHOOL DISTRICT, KATE BERNTSON

Some people think of Alaska's shape as a big, round pan, with the Southeast Region as the handle. That's why this region is often called the "Panhandle" of Alaska.

Southeast Region is a strip of mountainous islands and mainland about 600 miles long. To the west are the Gulf of Alaska and the Pacific Ocean. To the east are the St. Elias and Coast Mountains that separate the United States from Canada. Several rivers of the Panhandle, such as the Stikine near Wrangell, begin in Canada and drain through Southeast.

The southern half of the region's coast has hundreds of islands between the mainland and the Pacific Ocean. The protected channels between these islands form the Inside Passage. The area continues south to Dixon Extrance, a curve of water that forms the boundary between Alaska and Canada. Ships sailing south along this route connect Alaska to Canada and Washington state.

In the northern half of Southeast, there are few islands. The mainland is exposed to the ocean. Much of the area is rugged mountains and glaciers. Its shores are not protected from the pounding storms of the Gulf of Alaska. Fewer people live there than to the south.

R. E. JOHNSON

The Inside Passage provides sheltered waterways nearly all the way along the west coasts of Canada and Alaska. Alaska's portion, from Dixon Entrance to Skagway, is dotted with islands.

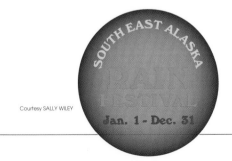

Southeast Alaska's wetlands and muskegs provide excellent breeding grounds for insects. In summer, being outdoors may mean putting up with clouds of mosquitoes, no see'ums, and black flies.

R. E. JOHNSON

Courtesy SALLY WILEY

2   The Weather

You will recall that Southeast Alaska has a Maritime climate. That means the climate is strongly affected by the ocean. As you remember, oceans moderate, or make less extreme, temperatures on land. Is the land cold? Oceans bring in warmer air. Is the land warm? Oceans bring in cooler air.

Islands are especially affected by oceans because they are surrounded by water. And what does Southeast Alaska have? That's right—plenty of islands. More than 1,000 islands rise from the sea here. Prince of Wales Island is the third largest in the United States. Only Kodiak and Hawaii are larger.

Most of the Southeast Region's weather comes from the ocean. That means rain, too. Clouds sweep in across the islands until they hit the Coast Mountains. Then they drop their moisture.

The capital city of Juneau gets about 100 inches of rain a year. Ketchikan gets more. Skagway gets less. You could guess that it rains in Southeast almost half the year at different times.

People joke about the rain. Somebody made up an annual Southeast Alaska "Rain Festival." No three-day celebration was this. The festival began January 1, and ended December 31.

Glaciers also affect the weather. Wherever they are found in Southeast Alaska, glaciers cool the air. Heavy, cold air sweeps down from them onto many parts of the region. Sometimes the air brings "Taku" winds (named for one of the glaciers), and they are—brrrr!—very cold.

Changeable weather such as fog, rain, snow, and wind affects the daily lives of people in the Southeast Region. Mail, supplies, and travelers sometimes cannot get to their destinations because of the weather. It stops planes from flying. It keeps boats from leaving docks.

A fourth grade student at Icy Bay, north of Yakutat, tells one way weather affects her part of Southeast:

You order food from a grocery store in Juneau by Fax on Monday, you get your food on Thursday by airplane. If there's lots of snow the plane cannot come or if the weather is bad. We would not be able to eat.

Icy Bay Community School. Teacher Adell Bruns

Drawing by Crissy Williquette, Icy Bay Community School. Teacher Adel Bruns

Planes generally save time for people, in spite of the weather. Consider this: It takes 40 minutes to fly from Port Alexander to Sitka. The same trip by boat takes about 10 hours!

3   The Glaciers

The landscape of Southeast Alaska was carved by ancient glaciers. Many glaciers still remain in the mountains, moving forward or melting back. One of the best places to see glaciers is Glacier Bay National Park.

What's In a Name?

Just as you have a name, you know that geographical places such as rivers, mountains, and villages have names, too. What your name is, and what it means, depends on what culture you come from.

Different cultures have different ways of naming places. The area now called Glacier Bay in Southeast Alaska is a good example.

Tlingit Indians who first lived in the area named places there for different reasons. Sometimes places were named for events that happened there, or for plants or animals that lived there. Or sometimes locations were named for natural changes taking place.

On the other hand, explorers coming later to Glacier Bay from other countries, named locations differently. They usually named places after people. Many times these were important people of the day. Sometimes locations were later named after the explorers themselves.

As an example, take the Tlingit Indian naming of an inlet *La.ayi Tukyee*, which means "glacier building the bay." In this naming, Natives tell what was happening there. When explorers came in the 1800s, they named this same place Muir Inlet after the naturalist John Muir.

S'aax X'aati is another case. In Tlingit this means "Marmot Island" and tells what animal lives there. When explorers came later, they named the same island Young Island in honor of the missionary S. Hall Young.

Lamplugh Glacier is named for the English geologist George W. Lamplugh, who visited Glacier Bay in 1884.

JIM HAUCK

Thousands of tourists visit the park every year, and scientists study how glaciers change the landscape.

Glaciers spread over the land farther north, too, past Yakutat to Icy Bay. The largest glacier in North America, the Malaspina, covers hundreds of square miles here. You might remember it was mentioned earlier in this book in the section on glaciers.

Mountains in the area, the St. Elias east of Yakutat, are still growing. Because of this, underground jolts can cause earthquakes in the area. One of the biggest quakes happened in September 1899. At that time, a prospector reported what happened to the Hubbard Glacier. He said, within five minutes the glacier "... ran out into the bay for half a mile..."

Another strong earthquake struck Lituya Bay in 1958. That quake caused land to slide from the mountain backing the bay. And talk about power! You might be used to seeing ocean waves a couple of feet high. The wave that splashed up from this slide shot more than 1,700 feet up the mountain slope. That's as high as four city street blocks placed end to end. That wave swept away trees like matchsticks.

It is interesting to know that, besides the mountains growing, land areas near Glacier Bay are also rising. Some land is rising as much as one inch a year. That's because as glaciers melt back, or retreat, they remove tremendous weight from the earth. It might be something like lifting a heavy brick or rock off a sponge. When the weight of the rock is removed, the sponge rises up.

PETER METCALFE

Besides glaciers, visitors to Glacier Bay may see icebergs, humpback whales, brown and black bears, lush rain forests, and up to 200 species of birds.

4   What Is There?

Once the glaciers melted back from Southeast Alaska after the Ice Age thousands of years ago, the animals and plants moved in.

Mild weather and heavy rains encouraged tree growth. The area was also too wet for wildfires, so some trees grew to be hundreds of years old. Plant communities grew thick beneath them. Mosses, ferns, devil's club, blueberries, and salmonberry bushes thrived.

USDA FOREST SERVICE, JUNEAU

Old-growth forests are more than big trees. Their complex living networks of plants, birds, insects, and other animals take hundreds of years to develop.

In winter, bald eagles from throughout Southeast Alaska gather in the Chilkat Valley near Haines. There may be more than 3,000 eagles there at one time.

ALASKA DIVISION OF TOURISM

Southeast Alaska contains some of the last great *old-growth forests* in the world. Today, bears use this old growth-forest for feeding and for winter dens. They feed on salmon that spawn in its streams. Bald eagles like to nest in its tall old spruce trees. Salmon enjoy the slow, shaded streams these old-growth forests provide.

These rainforests of spruce, cedar, and hemlock trees are part of the Tongass National Forest. This area is the largest forest controlled by the federal government in the United States. People have different ideas about how the forests should be used. There can be serious problems when some people want to keep the forests, and others want to cut them for timber. People have to work hard to decide what's best.

Southeast Alaska has more bald eagles than anywhere else in the world! Wolves and black bears thrive there, too. Except in one place. That's the "Alphabet Islands"—A̲dmiralty, B̲aranof, and C̲hichagof.

The ABC islands have deer and brown bears but no wolves or black bears. No one really knows why. Could it be there are enough huge brownies on the ABC's that other animals know to **STAY OUT?** Maybe that's it.

The land in Southeast Alaska supports a wealth of other animals besides bears, wolves, and deer. On the lowlands or in the mountains live mountain goats, porcupines, wolverines, foxes, martens, and moose.

The waters of Southeast Alaska are rich with an incredible menu of salmon, krill, crab, shrimp, halibut, and herring, stirred twice a day by the tide. Can there be any question why eagles, whales, seals, porpoises, sea lions, geese, and gulls come to dine? Of course, people fish there, too.

ALASKA DIVISION OF TOURISM

5 Moving Around in Southeast

Because of its islands and mountains, most of Southeast Alaska cannot be reached by roads. Haines, Skagway, and Hyder connect to highways, but other towns are reached only by plane or boat. That's how supplies are shipped in and out.

Since people need to move around and have connections with the world outside where they live, the State of Alaska operates a ferry system. This is called the Alaska Marine Highway. Seven large ships ferry tourists and residents, vehicles, and supplies among the communities of Southeast, and back and forth to Canada and Washington state.

In other places, students may take buses to basketball tournaments or for field trips. In Southeast Alaska, students often take the ferry.

As you can see, people move around in the Southeast Region, even though there are not many roads. Two

Humpback whales migrate from waters off Hawaii and Mexico each summer to feed in the productive waters of Southeast Alaska. Adult whales may be more than 40 feet long and weigh up to 35 tons.

Most towns in Southeast Alaska are reached by ferries of the Alaska Marine Highway. Tourists can ride the highway from Bellingham, Washington, all the way to Skagway.

ALASKA DIVISION OF TOURISM

STEVE KESSLER

Most of what moves in Petersburg is fishing boats. From the town, at the mouth of Wrangell Narrows, boats can reach many rich fishing grounds.

Fishing is a major industry in Southeast Alaska. Nowadays most fish is preserved by freezing.

ALASKA SEAFOOD MARKETING INSTITUTE

Petersburg students give a good idea of how people get from one place to another:

What moves in Petersburg?

Boats move!

Skiffs, fishing boats, kayaks, catamarans.

What moves in the air?

Airplanes on floats, snow, wind, rain, hail, clouds

helicopters, jets, sleet.

What moves on land?

Cars, hovercrafts, sleds, toboggans, B.M.W.s

Nathan Parker, Logan Durst,
Stedman Elementary School, Petersburg. Teacher Sally Riemer

However, there are roads in one part of Southeast Alaska—1,200 miles of roads open to the public. They're on Prince of Wales Island, where the El Capitan Caves are located. Most of the roads were built for logging. Now they are used by loggers, residents, and tourists visiting the island. All those roads made into one road would be enough for people to drive from Juneau to Barrow—clear across the state. It's the same distance.

6 Harvests from Land and Sea

Fishing is a main occupation in many towns in the Southeast Region. Salmon, halibut, herring, shrimp, and crab are caught and processed for sale or subsistence. In the forests and outside of towns, mining and logging are primary employers.

People have changed the land in many areas. Roads have been built to haul logs out. Acres of trees have been cut for construction and fuel. Towns have grown up to serve people who fish, settlers, government workers, business people, and their families. It has been happening for more than 100 years.

STEVE KESSLER

Settlements grow up for many reasons. Baranof Warm Springs has grown around the site of hot springs on Baranof Island.

Two students at Funter Bay on Admiralty Island told how the few people there have changed that corner of the world:

Over the years people have changed the land in Funter Bay by mining, developing a salmon cannery, building houses, planting gardens, and cutting down trees for firewood. We have cut down trees to clear a place for our house as well as to build wood sheds and shops. In planting gardens we take mud and sediment from the beaches and displace some of the sea creatures that might have otherwise been undisturbed, such as worms, small crabs, and eels. In mining people built roads, dug tunnels, dumped the tailings on the beaches, abandoned old equipment, and built railroads.

Megan and Gabe Emerson, Alyeska Central School. Teacher Debbie Chalmers

Not everyone likes the changes logging and mining have made. Some people say too many big old trees are being cut these days. Others are afraid that pollutants from mining could hurt people or disrupt the fisheries. Even visiting tourists can bring changes if there are thousands of them every year. People are working to make

DONNA EMERSON

Amid the ruins of an old cannery, two students from Funter Bay studied how people have changed the land near where they live. Gabe and Megan Emerson learned at home by correspondence through Alyeska Central School.

MARK KELLEY

Juneau, Alaska's capital city, clusters against the mountains along Gastineau Channel, part of the Inside Passage.

ALASKA DIVISION OF TOURISM, MARK WAYNE

a balance so there are jobs and the environment is safe at the same time.

7 Alaska's Capital City

Juneau, Alaska's capital, is the largest city in the region. It has about 30,000 residents. Juneau and its sister city of Douglas across Gastineau Channel stretch along the shore at the foot of mountains. Mendenhall Glacier, about 12 miles from town, is the only glacier in Southeast Alaska that can be reached by car.

The city started with gold mining in 1880. Later it was a stop-off for stampeders headed to Skagway for the Klondike Gold Rush. Now government and tourism are the main employers.

Since Juneau is the capital for Alaska, it is called "the seat of government." The elected head of Alaska, the governor, has offices and a home in Juneau.

Certain other Alaskans from all regions of the state are elected to travel to Juneau in the winter and spring. These people form the legislature, or the group that makes laws for the state. Using satellite television, faxes, computers, and other modern communications, these legislators keep

Alaska's legislature and governor have their offices in the Capitol Building in downtown Juneau.

in touch with their neighbors back home. They can talk instantly with the people who elected them in Wainright or Nenana or Klukwan. Keeping in contact is certainly different from what it was 50 years ago.

Juneau is also the headquarters for Sealaska Corporation. This Native regional corporation owns lands and businesses in Southeast Alaska. It promotes the interests and heritage of the native Tlingit and Haida people.

SEALASKA CORPORATION, MARK KELLEY

Sealaska Timber Corporation is Alaska's largest exporter of round logs. This shareholder/employee is loading milled lumber, possibly for shipment to East Asia.

8 The Towns of Southeast Alaska

More than 74,000 people live in Southeast Alaska. That's about one of every eight people in the state.

If you check a map, you will see just about all the towns in Southeast are on coastline or rivers. That includes the smaller towns such as Gustavus and Kake. Whether people live on the mainland or the islands, water provides most of their transportation, jobs, and food.

The fourth largest city in Alaska—Ketchikan—depends on the water for fishing, tourism, and transportation, too. Even nuclear submarines are seen passing by, as the U.S. Navy has a noise testing facility north of the city.

Ketchikan is called "The Gateway to Alaska" because it is the first port for ships sailing north. Besides fishing and private boats, tour ships, ferries, and airplanes bring several hundred *thousand* tourists to visit each year.

Many visitors first set foot in Alaska at Ketchikan, Alaska's "Gateway City" and its fourth largest.
ALASKA DIVISION OF TOURISM

Geography Sketch, 1892 Style

Throughout this book, you have read geosketches from students living now. Here is a geosketch written by someone more than a hundred years ago.

Louise Weeks was a young student at the Sitka Training School in 1892. She told about her village of Chilcat (now spelled Chilkat), south of Haines. The village was abandoned in 1910. This is how Louise felt about her home:

Chilcat is the most beautiful village I ever saw, with its broad beautiful river, and its mountains and hills. Many kinds of berries and fishes, sheep, and all kinds of birds are there. In summer people enjoy themselves going after berries with the children, men working at the fishes for winter, and other men go visiting Stick natives, from whom they brought so many queer things, also skulls and beautiful stones. Trees are different from other places in Alaska. All my family belong to Chilcat, only I was born in Sitka. Chilcat is ever so much colder than Sitka. The whole big river is frozen. All the people that are in Chilcat are to give thanks to God for the beautiful village and all the gifts of so many kinds of berries and all things.

From *The North Star,* Sitka, February 1892

Southeast does not have many roads, but Ketchikan's only highway is very busy. The road goes to a mall, the ferry dock, and the Native community of Saxman.

9   How Towns Grow

In small coastal towns, buildings are normally built along the waterfront, where most of the activity takes place. There's usually one main road.

In larger towns, streets often grew from walking trails of earlier days. These trails were

JIM HAUCK

widened for horses, then carts, then cars. Now some of them are roads or small highways. You can tell they are old roads because they are often curved or winding rather than straight.

You can tell a lot about the town's history from street names, too, If you hear names like Stedman or Kowee or Zimovia or Egan for your streets, your history book can tell you the rest of the story.

Sometimes you can tell how a town has grown over the years by its cemeteries. In early days, burial grounds were outside of town. They were away from the homes and businesses. As people moved in the town grew, and people built around the cemeteries. To a newcomer arriving in a large town, it may seem as though the cemetery was placed in the middle of town.

However it was not planned that way from the beginning.

Sitka's cemetery is like that, and so is Juneau's.

Look where the cemetery is in your town, and you could get an idea of how the area has grown.

While you are looking at cemeteries, notice some of the old headstones and markers. They tell you a lot about what happened in the town over the years. They also tell you who helped build the town into the busy place it is today.

Like the rest of Alaska, the Southeast Region has a long history. Geography shaped the land thousands of years ago. Native people and later newcomers populated the area, each bringing their ways and cultures. Today visitors from other places come to Southeast to view the geography and to experience this mix of cultures.

JIM HAUCK

Every town is filled with clues about its history, including Sitka, where a monument reminds people of Alaska's Gold Rush pioneers.

Suggested Reading

Dowd, John. *Ring of Tall Trees.* Anchorage: Alaska Northwest Books, 1992.
> A young boy helps protect an ancient forest in British Columbia from being logged.

Hoyt-Goldsmith, Diane. *Totem Pole.* N.Y.: Holiday House, 1990.
> A Tsimshian Indian boy proudly describes how his father carved a totem pole for the Klallam tribe, and the subsequent celebration.

Rand, Gloria. *Salty Sails North.* N.Y.: Henry Holt Co., 1990.
> Salty Dog and Zack sail north to Alaska, encountering other ships, a storm, and wild animals on the shore.

Sattler, Helen Roney. *The Book of Eagles.* N.Y.: Lothrop, Lee & Shepard Books, 1989.
> Describes physical characteristics, behavior, and life cycle of eagle species around the world—including the bald eagle.

JIM HAUCK

Totems reflect the Tlingit heritage of much of Southeast Alaska

North to the Future

Like the astronaut in the beginning of the book, you, too, have seen an overview of Alaska now.

In this geography book, you traveled through time from the earliest beginnings of Alaska. You saw how Alaska was formed, and why people came to the "Great Land." You saw how Alaska's land, water, and air shape the way people live, how they move around, and why they come and go. Perhaps you got a sense of how people's feelings for the land bind them to the past and to the future. And you saw how Alaska fits with other places on earth.

The whole world has changed in that time, too. The world is no longer made up of far off countries. Fast transportation and communications link nations in hours or minutes. People travel and move with ease. It might be better to think of countries as neighboring towns, only hours or minutes away. A change to one "town" affects all the others.

Alaska is one of those neighbors. Alaska's motto, "North to the Future," perhaps means more now than in the past. Whereas Alaska was once thought of as a cold, far-off place, it has now

JODY MARCELLO

The world seems smaller as teachers from Alaska and other parts of the United States visit with students in Russia.

BILL MARTIN-MUTH

Kidlink Circles the Globe

During the 1990 Gulf War in Iraq, CNN Communications was telling the world what was happening there. At the same time, students in Israel were sending out messages from basement computers. Pupils at Nordale Elementary School in Fairbanks got the messages.

All those boys and girls were on the Internet group called *Kidlink*, a worldwide computer network. It's strictly for kids from 10 to 15 years old. Other than some supervision, it's "no adults allowed." Nordale pupils have talked to students in Israel, Iceland, Norway—actually, on all the continents. Most students who exchange electronic mail know enough English to get by, so language is seldom a problem.

Students used to write letters to *pen pals* in other countries. Now they link up with *keypals* on the computer. What do they talk about? Everything from world peace to soccer to just making friends. As time goes by, students all over the world may have their own e-mail addresses.

become an important focus. Many world jobs and businesses have shifted to nations along the Pacific Ocean—the Pacific Rim. And with jobs and businesses come people, of course. Alaskan towns now see families from other countries working and living in the Great Land.

There is also exchange with school classes in other lands. Students in Japan, for instance, are just a phone, a fax, or a computer away.

In a few years you will be in high school. What more changes will there be in those years, and in you?

Think about how geography changes and how people change, even as you look out the window of your school classroom.

The future of Alaska is you. You are part of it all.

Suggested Reading

Murphy, Claire Rudolf. *Friendship Across Arctic Waters.* N.Y.: Lodestar Books, 1991.

> Describes the field trip of 11 Cub Scouts from Alaska to Provideniya, a small town in the Soviet Far East.

Glossary

alpine tundra: tundra found in the mountains above treeline

Antarctic Circle: the line of latitude 66 1/2 degrees south of the Equator. Every place south of this line receives one or more days of continuous light during the antarctic summer.

Arctic Circle: the line of latitude 66 1/2 degrees north of the Equator. Every place north of this line receives one or more days of continuous light during the arctic summer.

axis: an imaginary line showing the angle at which the earth tilts as it travels around the sun

boom: a period of time when many people move into an area to make great profits from developing a resource

boreal forest: the forest found in the earth's colder regions. This forest has only a few varieties of trees. Spruce are the typical *coniferous,* or needle-leafed, trees; and birch are the typical *deciduous,* or broad-leafed, trees. In summer the area may have many forest fires.

camouflage: a disguise—often a color or a pattern—that an animal uses to hide from or fool another animal

chill factor: a combination of temperature and wind speed that is colder than the same temperature without wind. Also called *windchill.*

climate: a description of overall weather conditions in an area over a period of many years

continental shelf: gently sloping land at the edges of continents that is covered by shallow ocean water. Most of the ocean plant and animal life is found here.

corporations (Alaska Native): organizations formed under the Alaska Native Claims Settlement Act (ANCSA) to serve Native people and manage the land and money they received under the Act

culture: the way of life of a group of people. The group has a common language, set of beliefs, and shared customs.

environment: everything around a particular person or place

Equator: the line of 0 degrees latitude that extends around the widest part of the earth. It is halfway between the North and South Poles.

eruption: the explosion of gases, ash, and molten rock from a volcano

fault zone: a break or crack in the earth's crust where earthquakes are likely to take place

ROGER W. PEARSON

geography: the study of the earth and the living things on it

ice floe: a large piece of floating ice several feet to a few miles across

ice-wedge polygons: patterns in the ground caused by permafrost activity

igloo: an Eskimo house or dwelling (*iglu*), often shaped like a dome, usually made of sod, wood, stone, or snow

Inside Passage: the protected waterway between the mainland and offshore islands along the northwest coast of the United States and Canada

kayak: a canoe made of a frame completely covered with skins except for an opening in the top where a person can sit

latitude: distance north or south of the Equator. It is measured in degrees and minutes.

longitude: distance east or west of the prime (or zero) meridian. It is measured in degrees and minutes.

mantle: the layer of hot, molten rock that lies between the earth's hard outer crust and its hot, inner core

meridian: an imaginary line of measurement running north and south on the earth's surface. Also called a line of longitude.

midden: a heap of material thrown away by a person or a group of people

migration: movement from place to place; for animals, usually according to the season or time of year

moraine: piles or mounds of stones, sand, and soil left behind by a glacier

muskeg: flat, boggy ground that has thick layers of peat or decayed plants underneath. Usually small ponds and stunted evergreen trees are scattered throughout.

old-growth forests: forests hundreds of years old that have trees of various sizes and ages, and a variety of plants growing beneath them

USDA FOREST SERVICE, JUNEAU

pack ice: sea ice that is floating free and may be moved by wind and currents. It grows larger in winter and smaller in summer, but some always remains in the Arctic Ocean.

parallel: an imaginary line of measurement running east to west on the earth's surface. Also known as a line of latitude.

60° N
20° N
0°
150° W
120° W
90° W
60° W
30° W
20° S
60° S
North Pole
Equator - 0° Latitude
South Pole

197

peninsula: land that is surrounded by water on all but one side

permafrost: ground that is frozen all year long. Many parts of Alaska have permafrost. The top, or *active,* layer will thaw and then freeze again as the weather changes. The *inactive* layer stays frozen all the time.

pictograph: a simple ancient drawing that tells a story

pingo: a large mound formed when water under the soil freezes and bulges upward. Pingos are found where lakes used to be.

plateau: a broad, flat area of land that is 1,000 or more feet higher than sea level

plate tectonics: movement of the floating plates, or pieces, of the earth's crust

predator: an animal that hunts other animals for food

prey: an animal that is hunted by other animals for food

rainforests: areas where trees and the plants beneath them flourish because of plentiful rain

spawning: the process of producing, laying, and fertilizing eggs, especially in fish

subsistence: living by depending on what is in the environment around you, rather than bringing in food or other necessities from another place.

thaw lakes: shallow lakes formed by the melting of ground ice. They are usually round or oblong in shape.

tsunami: a wave or wall of water caused by an earthquake

tundra: the cold, treeless landscape found in northern regions

vapor: the gaseous form of a substance such as water

volcano: a crack in the earth's crust from which steam and melted rock erupt. Volcanoes are cone-shaped.

weather: the state of the air outdoors at a particular time

MARK AND AUDREY HODGINS

Index

Melanie Kulukhon and Stacey Uglowook,
Gambell Elementary School.

May all my small mistakes
go into their places
and make little noise.

—*Traditional Eskimo saying (N.W.F)*